UNDER WATER

Claire Walsh is a freediver, year-round sea swimmer and teacher of breathwork courses. She was the first person to represent Ireland at the Freediving World Championships in 2019. Born and raised in landlocked Kildare, she now lives by the coast with her husband, Boudy.

UNDER WATER

HOW HOLDING MY BREATH TAUGHT ME TO LIVE

CLAIRE WALSH

GILL BOOKS

Gill Books
Hume Avenue
Park West
Dublin 12
www.gillbooks.ie

Gill Books is an imprint of M.H. Gill and Co.

978 07171 9486 5

Designed by Bartek Janczak
Edited by Emma Dunne
Proofread by Ciara McNee
Printed and bound by Scandbook, Sweden
This book is typeset in 11.5 on 16.5pt, Sabon.

The paper used in this book comes from the wood pulp of sustainably managed forests.

A CIP catalogue record for this book is available from the British Library.

5 4 3 2 1

Some names and identifying details have been changed to protect the privacy of the people involved.

For Mum and Dad

‘When you find yourself alone in a silent underwater world, you’ll reconsider your previous thoughts and attitudes, and discover new things. Thoughts pass and disappear in a few seconds, and this silence has a calming and nurturing effect on our restless souls.’

Natalia Molchanova, world champion freediver (1962–2015)

CONTENTS

PROLOGUE

Underwater you don't hear anything.

Putting my face in the water is like a sigh of relief for my mind. Internal chatter, judgements and criticism fade to a white noise and the rhythmic anchor of my breathing through the snorkel lulls me into the welcomed quietness.

Dancing in front of my eyes, beams of light extend 30 metres below me, showcasing a spectrum of silvers, blues and greens. She's in a playful mood today, the sea. Winking at me, beckoning me, her flirtatiousness belies her strength. I smile back and she sends a wave to flood my snorkel. Purging my snorkel, I exhale forcefully. Okay, okay! I never was in any doubt who was boss.

I settle into my breathe up, the preparation, the cycle of breathing to bring the body and mind into a state of relaxation before a dive. This sound, the slight dragging of the air through the snorkel, amplified by my neoprene hood and the water, is one I dream about when lying in bed. When sleep evades me, I think of this moment, this soothing lullaby, and just as in the water, my eyelids grow heavier and my limbs soften. This is, after all, an extreme sport of relaxation.

My dive today is 60 metres. This is my deepest dive. The line is lowered and set, the depth marked out by pieces of red electrical tape in a series of lines. At the bottom, above the weight, the bottom plate is waiting for me at the target depth with a little Velcro tag that I'll tuck in my hood and bring back up as a souvenir, proof that I've reached my goal.

In the broader world of competitive freediving, 60 metres isn't deep – not by a long shot. The world record for women in this discipline, free immersion, is 98 metres. But it's deep for me, a personal best in fact.

I once described my goal of diving 60 metres to my friend, Máirín, quickly following it up with the customary disclaimer that it isn't really *that* deep for a freediver. I proceeded to rattle off the world records, as well as how much deeper friends of mine dived, with each number diminishing my own achievement, desperate for her to understand that this wasn't *deep* deep.

Some months later Máirín and I took a spin into town. We parked in the centre of Dublin city, and I started to head in the direction of the restaurant.

'Nope, this way first.' Máirín cocked her head and set off in the opposite direction. I rolled my eyes, not in the mood to play along. Where were we going? I was hungry.

We rounded the corner and came to the base of Liberty Hall.

'How tall is it again?'

'Fifty-nine metres,' I whispered.

'Fifty-nine metres,' she repeated.

We stood looking, craning our necks to see the top of the building outlined against the grey sky above.

'Don't ever try and convince me that's not an achievement, Claire Walsh.'

I nodded silently. Sixty metres no longer felt small.

Floating on the surface of the water I try not to imagine an inverted Liberty Hall lying beneath me, waiting to be scaled on one breath. Instead, I lift the corners of my mouth to a gentle smile and visualise the dive ahead of me. Peeking through half-closed eyes, I catch sight of those winking, twinkling beams. *You've got this*, the sea whispers.

Setting off with purpose, this is softer than concentration. This is focus, this is trust, this is my mind stepping to the side and allowing my body to trigger the physiological responses that we humans share with dolphins, whales and seals. While 3 minutes underwater to 60 metres and 7 atmospheres of pressure sounds extreme, I have trained my dive reflex. I trust my body and make the adaptations to protect my ears from the increase in pressure, my lungs from the weight of the water around me, to conserve energy and use my precious oxygen efficiently. And when the levels of CO_2 in my blood rise and I get that urge to breathe, I trust my mind to find ease beyond the discomfort to allow me to continue on my 60-metre odyssey.

Pulling myself down the rope, head first with my feet trailing behind me, I remind myself how lucky I am to be doing this. I close my eyes and settle into the pull, pull, pull rhythm. My jaw makes the smallest of adjustments as I equalise my ears against the pressure of this dense first 10 metres. My environment begins to fade into the darker colours of the quieter underwater world; my movements, pace and reactions must be measured and match.

Efficiency is key.

Then something magical starts to happen. The space between each pull opens up: pull and glide, pull and glide. I've moved through the axis from being positively buoyant, through neutral and into the delicious sinking freefall of negative buoyancy. In that glide there's a sense of breaking through, of release. The glides stretch further still and it makes me think that this is the closest I'll get to flying. Peter Pan sort of flying. Second-star-to-the-right sort of flying, effortless soaring-through-the-clouds freedom. The caress of the water on my skin not covered by my wetsuit is all that reminds me that I'm not in the clouds, I'm underwater ... but still flying.

The increasing pressure all around – the weighted compression of my chest, the mask being pushed back into my face – lets me know I am sinking. I don't need to open my eyes to the hazy dark-green surroundings to know that I'm getting deeper. Careful not to make any big movements, I send one last reminder through my body to soften, relaxing my feet, releasing tension from my knees, my belly, my neck. This is my favourite part of the dive: freefall. Light, sounds and the surface have faded. To be here, at this depth, is both incredibly empowering and completely humbling. Pulling my focus inwards, swaddled in this state between awake and asleep, I let go and savour the experience.

Touchdown.

I'm here already? Freefall had passed in a dreamy blur and I was at the bottom. My lanyard carabiner hits the stopper and I reach below to take a tag from the bottom plate. I've made it! I allow the smallest, split second of celebration before turning and tucking the little piece of Velcro into my hood. Now for the way back up. I don't think about racing to the surface or a need to breathe. Out of the corner of my eye I catch the yawning black hole in the coral to my right, locally known as the Arch. I nod, somewhat respectfully, and I settle into a steady, efficient pace that moves me out of the enveloping pressure of depth. The mantra *you've got this, you've got this, you've got this* helps create a rhythm to my pulls, but more importantly keeps my mind anchored and stops it straying down any unhelpful mental paths. Thoughts use oxygen too and, as I said, the name of the game is efficiency.

I know there's a risk involved. To the uninitiated, freediving seems extreme at best and downright dangerous at worst. Often considered one of the most dangerous sports in the world, I've heard it being described as 'basically scuba-diving but without the apparatus'. Looking at it that way, taking a deep breath and going down on just the air in your lungs, pulling down on a rope or swimming down as far as you can and then having to come all the way back up, it sounds utterly stressful and even panic-inducing. It doesn't sound just dangerous but complete lunacy.

There is a risk, but it's a calculated risk. I know the rules; I am under the watchful eye of my coach, my safety diver. I'm attached to the line by my lanyard. I am doing all I can to keep myself safe. In doing that, I can put the risk out of my mind and focus on the upside: the relaxation.

A unique form of relaxation, freediving to me is a negotiation between body and mind, a quest for a state that requires confidence and concentration, as well as humility and softness. It pierces through surface layers and works with you on a level of intimacy that day-to-day living rarely affords. Striving to hit that balance is like juggling self-awareness, autonomy and trust.

Right on cue, my safety diver appears in my field of vision. I ease into a pull and glide and allow my gaze to take in my surroundings. I notice the changes in light, the colours of the coral along the walls in front of me and take a quick mental picture of how incredible this journey back up looks.

Approaching the last 10 metres of the dive, also known as the low O_2 zone, I gently repeat to myself what I'm going to do once I reach the surface. *Breathe, remove mask, signal 'okay', say 'I'm okay'*. Ten metres to the surface is where most shallow-water blackouts occur. Here divers experience a sudden drop in partial pressure of oxygen in the lungs. With my coach watching my ascent, I feel safe and focus on my surface protocol.

Breathe. Mask. Signal. 'I'm okay.'

I break the surface and drape my arms over the buoy as I take some active recovery breaths.

'Breathe, Claire,' my coach reminds me softly, positioning himself so he can see my face and watch for signs of hypoxia. I know I'm fine – 'perfectly clean' – as we freedivers say. Catching my breath, I remove my mask, wipe the water off my face, signal towards him and say, 'I'm okay.' I keep breathing and pull my tag from my hood. The buoy erupts in splashes – the customary celebration in freediving. It's taken me so long to get here, not just to this depth, but to the trust, the appreciation for each moment and the ability to find moments of relaxation amid discomfort. It is indeed worthy of celebration.

Dipping my head below the buoy to detach my

lanyard, I look down at where I've just returned from. I think of the fear that a few years earlier would have stopped me attempting such a feat and how much I'd have missed out on, not just in the achievement but, like most things, the process to get here.

Freediving has brought me around the world, allowed me to explore underwater scenes that would rival anything from *Finding Nemo* and created a network and sense of belonging with those that I trust with my life, my freediving buddies. Most importantly, it has nurtured a dialogue, a much-needed mediation between my mind and my body, facilitated by the wisest of teachers, the Breath. It has initiated me into the world of mindfulness: being fully immersed in the moment, without judgement or expectation. Something that had evaded me on land for years.

So what's it like to take part in the second most dangerous sport in the world? In this extreme sport of relaxation, I haven't endangered my life, but learned how to live it.

Take a deep breath. Concentrate. Allow your shoulders to fall away from your ears and instead stack the air in your belly, your ribcage expanding confidently, your chest welcoming the stretch. Imagine a wave of oxygen flowing, undulating up your spine and awakening your body as it moves through you. Pausing at the top of the inhale you feel full, fuller than you've experienced before. Heart beating against your lower ribs, fingertips tingling with life, your face feels a flash of heat. Smile, get comfortable, be prepared to meet yourself, become reacquainted with yourself and learn that you are capable of more than you anticipated. It's this pause, this place, this unexplored playground between the inhale and the exhale where the magic is going to happen.

Let's dive right in.

chapter 1

WHAT DO YOU DO?

Are you still watching?

Hitting 'continue', I couldn't have told you what had happened in the previous episode – or the one before that if I was being honest. I just needed something to go in front of my eyes, a distraction, white noise.

'Are you getting up today?' Mum popped her head in the door, hoover in hand, the smell of lemon floor cleaner wafting upstairs. Monday is 'chore day', always has been.

'Not for a while,' I replied somewhat sheepishly, feeling like a lazy teen who grumbles about having to get out of bed at midday. But I was 32, it was 10 a.m. and my day off.

The innocuous exchange left me feeling anxious and not a little bit guilty. *I should be* – I caught myself.

Should.

It was a sticking point for me, a word I battled with and against on a daily basis. On my day off I *should* really give myself a break. Shite, there I went again.

I was back living at home. I had spent the last few years renting, sometimes building a home and other times paying money to condense my life, my living, to a damp single bedroom. Living at the behest of landlords was restrictive at best, and each time my housemates and I received the 'one month's notice: we intend to sell/move back into the property' email, it sent us into a tailspin. Downloading Daft and setting up viewings, searching our emails for the references and documents we'd assembled only months previously. Then to packing, pulling out the cardboard IKEA boxes from storage. You had intended to throw them out last time but stopped yourself, not fully confident you wouldn't need them again in the near future. Each attempt to find a new dwelling was a race, a competitive one at that, and handicaps like, for example, receiving that mail on 18 December told you that your odds weren't very good. You'd need a place for an interim stay. That's how I found myself boomeranging back to my childhood bedroom.

The household sounds – the creak of the third stair, the *Morning Ireland* music and the kettle boiling – were both comforting and suffocating. I felt like a failure. Mum and Dad were gracious, welcoming, and facilitated the change, but there was no getting around the fact that I was an adult living in another adult's house and that it was just as hard on them as it was on me. Having my way of living, my adult patterns and routines, replanted into this new–old environment made me feel caged in and exposed. My chest tightened and my skin itched with a sense of restlessness and unease. I was all over the place, literally. At the bottom of my bed was a bag for the week crammed with notes, materials, changes of clothes, empty and stained travel mugs and the inevitable apple I had forgotten about. My clothes were in a suitcase in the corner. Unpacking and hanging my clothes in the wardrobe that I had, in my teens, covered in glow-in-the-dark stars was too much of an admission that I'd be here for a while, that I was officially back living with my parents. The boot of my car had boxes of my belongings that came with me on my commute, with the remainder stacked in a damp corner in the puppet theatre. This temporary way of living was surreptitiously morphing into the norm, leaving me feeling unanchored and unsettled. I quashed these emotions by keeping on the move: teaching, performing and belting it across the M50 to get from one job to the other. I'd keep going, another quick cup of coffee and a chocolate bar for sustenance, the nervous energy fuelling my commute that criss-crossed Kildare and Dublin multiple times a day.

Until I stopped. My days off saw me feeling spent, drained.

I was unrecognisable from the person who stood tall, confident and assured and animatedly addressed the 50 people in front of her. She felt far away at those moments. It was too much – I needed to switch off, dull my senses and recharge. If I could just turn my brain off and rest …

My working week started on a Wednesday. Banging on the door of the bathroom, begging my brother to hurry up. I'd miss my shower window because of the repeated snooze button. I'd grab a quick rinse, more so to wake me up and help cleanse the cloud of grogginess that wrapped around me like the steam of the bathroom. No time for luxuries like breakfast, make-up or dry hair, I'd slop coffee into a travel mug and hit the road.

One of my jobs was teaching drama in a primary school. The 30-minute slots felt unnecessarily like torture. I'd been there years, seen the kids go from adorable full-cheeked junior infants to sullen but *very* cool pre-teens. The teachers were polite, and some were friendly, but I felt out of place among them, not a *real* teacher. I'd long since given up on going to the staff room, instead skipping lunch or munching on an apple in the too hot or too cold (but never *juuuust* right) drama room.

It was five hours of being 'on'. Some days I managed, lifting the class with my enthusiasm and excitement, relishing their creativity. Other days I felt like a shell, barely able to summon the energy to smile. Those days I felt disappointed in myself, inadequate, and silently promised myself to do better the next week.

The next few days would pass in a blur of smiling, singing, performing, cursing at traffic, anxious glances at clocks and hurried meals shovelled into my mouth while hopping from one foot to the other. I'd stretched myself way too thin. I'd swallow another mouthful of coffee, plaster a smile onto my face and will my energy to keep going just a *little bit* longer. Hoping to pull off that swan gliding-on-the-water look while swimming like fuck underneath the surface. Maybe it was time to face facts: my swan was more wobble than glide … and she was not a very good swimmer.

◆ ◆ ◆

Lengthening my spine, I took a deep breath and pulled open the door to the bar. *Shit, what's his name again?* Rummaging for my phone, I opened the app: Mark, grand. At the same time, a message came in to let me know he's running a bit late. It was always the greeting bit that I got nervous about. Should I go in for a cheek kiss? Is a hug overfamiliar? I had a guy stretch his hand out like he was meeting a prospective employer. That was weird. I suppose it *was* an interview of sorts.

Mark's missed bus gave me a chance to get settled. I ordered a G&T without the G to disguise the fact that I wasn't drinking. Turns out Leixlip wasn't a very *sexy* place to live, and especially not when you were driving 40 minutes back to it and *it* was your parents' house. I slid my car keys off the table and into my handbag and positioned myself to be able to see Mark make his grand entrance.

Oh sweet Jesus, I can't believe I put on a full face of make-up for this. Lipstick, I'm wearing LIPSTICK, for feck's sake.

I smiled and listened to him describe his perfect woman: petite, 'up for the craic' and brunette. Oh, and big boobs, as he winked lavishly at me. Terrific, I'd hit one on the list, possibly two. Yay me?

His last girlfriend was a model, did I know that? Funnily enough, no, I didn't. Please tell me more about her. Sex mad was she? Oh, how lovely for her. Couldn't drive the length of the M50 without pulling in and giving you a – OKAY! I get the idea, thanks. You wouldn't catch *her* dead on a dating app? Ah right, was that because of the 'model status', do you think?

'So Claire, what do *you* do?'

Hands down, this was my least favourite question. Heck, I was even guilty of asking it myself from time to time. Unable to catch the words before they were out of my mouth, I would kick myself, knowing that I'd have to answer the same question.

'Ahm – well, it depends on what day of the week it is ...'

And maybe what time of the year it was and *which* year it was. I wasn't trying to be deliberately obtuse or evasive. When it came to my work, it just wasn't a straightforward question.

Undeterred, he kept going: ‘Have you had many long-term relationships? Do you have kids? Are you renting or have you bought?’

‘Yes. Nope. Nope – I mean, renting. Well, not quite renting. I *was* renting and now I’m back with my parents ...’

I trailed off and let the silence hang in the air as his eyebrows furrowed. I could see him mentally scanning box labels, trying to figure out which one to put me in.

Single?

Living with her parents.

No kids.

She must be really focused on her career then.

‘So, what is it that you actually do?’

Aaaand we were right back to where we started.

‘I do a lot of things. I sing. I swim in the sea, all year round. I work as a puppeteer’ – cue him, as everyone did, making sock-puppet hand gestures and me (mentally) replying with a different kind of hand gesture – ‘I work as a drama teacher, a singing teacher, a movement teacher and occasionally a movement director. I run choirs, gospel choirs, choirs for fun, and I’ve taught people about breathing and how to use their voice. I sometimes run workshops and I sometimes put on shows.’

I could tell people what I did, but it would always come with a disclaimer.

When I was studying for my Leaving Cert, it was coming up to my practical singing exam in music. I went to meet the pianist accompanying me to go over my piece a week before the exam. I handed over my sheet music, took a drink of water and cleared my throat before apologising.

'You'll have to excuse me, I have a bit of a sore throat at the moment.'

He didn't sympathise, offer me a Strepsil or advise a complicated steam and eucalyptus routine for later. He merely scoffed, maybe even snorted, and replied, 'You and every other singer I've played with.'

That was my introduction to the disclaimer: a rush of words that you offer preceding a task to help others manage their expectations of you. An excuse. A self-deprecating babble. A warning. An explanation.

My answer to *What do you do* was always preceded by my disclaimer: a well-rehearsed and slick piece with interchangeable phrases to suit the situation – and delivered with a smile. What no one would know was that it continued for *way longer* in my head once I'd finished the verbal part. Smile gone, this next, internal phase was where things became less structured. Thoughts picked up pace as punctuation took its leave. Words leapfrogged over one another narrating an imagined dialogue with a building sense of urgency.

Maybe it started off as an attempt to cultivate an 'Ah sure, look' free-spirited approach to life or to mask a vulnerability or provide a justification. Or maybe it was because when it came to what I did, I felt a little bit ashamed and, a lot of the time, embarrassed.

Swirling the ice cubes left at the bottom of my empty glass, I left my mouth on 'automatic response' while my brain struck through the hopeful scenarios I had in my head. *Jesus, I don't know what's more pathetic at this stage – the fact that I still hold out hope for each first date or the fact that I probably will go on a second date with him ...*

Women in their 30s are dangerous. Perceived as a predatory bunch, sniffing out partners with frantic urgency underscored by the ominous ticking of their biological clocks ... Or so our 'I'm not ready to settle down yet' counterparts would have us think. It felt like the trickiest of balancing acts, to want, maybe even yearn, for a partner but to still appear aloof, to be aware of your age, acknowledging and respecting any desire to have a family in the future, but to be 'chill' and nonchalant about wanting something serious. Just be yourself but don't give too much away. Know who you are and what you want but don't scare him with your independence. Online dating felt more and more like a game: scoring points, collecting weapons, avoiding traps until you qualified for the next level ... and then do it all again. It was trying to figure out a set of rules that you'd been handed, that you didn't know exactly how much you agreed with, but you'd been told that *it's all part of the game*. For better or worse, you'd decided to play.

I'd had relationships, even long-term ones. I was someone who saw myself meeting a guy, walking down the aisle, right, together, left, together, buying a house and having kids. Sure I'd work, but to be fair, having studied drama and done a master's in movement, the details of that career path was always a bit hazy. My relationship goals were all pretty much 'tick the boxes'. At 28 I found myself newly single and a bit dazed by the prospect that my life might not look like I had always thought. I wasn't quite ready to reimagine a new path nor was I excited by the potential. Quite the opposite. I was scared; I was embarrassed. The 'how things should be done' blinkers were firmly in place, my naivety limiting my imagination. I couldn't envisage a life beyond that and I didn't know where to start.

So in my 20s, I had profiles on POF, Match, Tinder and Bumble. The more I chased the original 'plan', the further away it seemed. I wouldn't say that I was – that dirtiest of dirty words in the dating game – desperate – but I was the *other* dirty word: lonely. It's not like I didn't enjoy my own company; I could go to a restaurant on my own, for coffee, to the cinema. I'm great company and entertain myself no end. But I felt like I didn't fit in with my peers among the engagement/new house/promotion celebrations. Now I was 32, single, couldn't rent, let alone buy, my own place and my work, although rewarding in the moment, wasn't on a solid career trajectory ... and had me physically and mentally all over the shop. I felt like there was a huge new checklist and I just couldn't get my shit together enough to tick even one of them off.

I was a reluctant 'free spirit' square peg in a 'settling down' round hole. No matter how I squashed and pushed and yearned for it, I just couldn't seem to fit. I was exhausted. I needed more than this. I wanted more than this.

♦ ♦ ♦

It started off as a musing over Christmas. 'I think I might go travelling through South America,' I announced, testing how it sounded out loud. My brother, Matt, had spent a few months travelling the summer before and had planted the seed of the idea. It was peak pantomime season in the puppet theatre and with each 'oh yes you did' and 'it's BEHIND YOU', I was inching closer to saying 'feck it!' and packing my bags. It's not that I had a huge urge to travel but more a huge need for change – a change of scenery was as good a thing as the next. It wasn't going to fix things – where I live, what I do and who, in the future, I might do it with. It was an escape, a knee-jerk reaction, a forceful kicking down of the walls that I felt were moving in on me, an attempt to create space. To breathe.

I hadn't done the 'year out to travel' in my 20s like many of my friends had. I was too busy. I spent most of my 20s playing hide-and-seek with depression, putting my hands over my eyes, and like a toddler's idea of 'hiding', hoping it wouldn't find me. Spoiler: it did.

I've used the same analogy for years to describe depression. It starts with:

It's like you're playing baseball.

This in itself is gas. Not only do I know very little about sport in general but I know absolutely feck all about baseball. I went to watch games (Games? Matches? ... See what I mean!) when on holidays but all I remember are the snacks and the songs; both excellent.

It's like you're playing baseball and are at home base. Then something happens, disorients you, and when you go to place your foot on home base, it's been moved. You're no longer safe and, try as you might, your foot can never find that spot.

I don't know how well this ties in with the actual rules of baseball or whether I'm merging them with the made-up rules we imposed for playing rounders as kids. But what I was trying to describe was the sense of never knowing, never trusting what you thought you knew, what had been familiar and safe.

Sure, there's sadness, unexplainable sadness, weighty pressing-on-your-chest sort of sadness. But worse than the sadness is the nothingness. Numb, unfeeling. Despondent, unable to feel fear or anxiety but also joy, excitement ... or peace. There's the tiredness that makes mountains out of the smallest of tasks and that can, in an instant, flip into restlessness that has you afraid to stay still.

I think, if I had thought about it long enough, I might have guessed these were symptoms of depression.

What I would never have expected was the guilt. Not only do you feel this way but it's compounded by an unbearable guilt *for* feeling this way. Compared to others, your life is charmed, uncomplicated and so privileged. How dare you – what right have you to feel like this? Pull yourself together, think positively, go for a walk – snap out of it.

But I wasn't just *looking for attention* and, try as I might, attempts to snap out of it resulted in a mounting pressure to hide it. I could feel it ... even before I opened my eyes in the morning. It was a heaviness that waited behind my eyes – it didn't matter whether they were open or closed.

Waking was either one of two things.

Eyelids shooting open, unsure of whether I was even asleep to begin with. My phone would let me know that a few hours had passed but also that it was too early to get up. I needed to get back to sleep. I needed to get back to sleep before my brain, those thoughts, stirred. Rolling over with a quiet caution, I would repeat *go back to sleep, go back to sleep* to myself like an urgent prayer. I needed to go back to sleep before I was caught.

Too late.

Lying down, the tears would slide down each side of my face, as if running away from each other. I tried to take a deep breath against the gulps of panic tightening my throat, my chest heaving as short and shallow breaths threatened to engulf me. I lay still. *I need to ride this out. I know the drill.*

I'd long since lost trust in my own judgement and my own emotions as being reliable barometers of any given situation. So I found myself reverting to people who could speak louder, more confidently, seem more assured, to help create my own sense of self, my own recollection of situations. Thoughts and memories mixed and merged, sliding over one another, distorting, warping. With each one I was brought back to events, conversations where a new meaning, a new version revealed itself. And with each retelling the actual people involved fell away and they became stock characters, personas that hissed in my ear, telling me I'm not good enough, that I'm wrong, unkind, ugly, selfish, cruel, fat and failing in everything that I do and unlovable in everything that I am. Each new thought spiderwebbed out into 12 more, each as virulent as the next, triggering waves of anger, shame, hatred and fear. Time, counselling and daylight hours would remind me that this wasn't *truth*: it was an onslaught of my demons, taking advantage of my sleeping state to catch up on me. They'd be gone in the morning.

But I was scared.

Do you remember that scene in *Willy Wonka and the Chocolate Factory*, the version with Gene Wilder in it, when the lucky visitors have stuffed their gobs with giant gummy bears, edible toadstools and lollipops the size of tennis rackets, and now stand in confusion beside the chocolate river having witnessed Augustus Gloop's demise. Wonka, seemingly impervious to the recent events, gestures to a delightful-looking steamboat that emerges from a tunnel to take them on the next part of their tour.

Wonka eases their fears, reassuring them that they're going to love this, and to start with they do. Cheerfully setting off, this is simply the next part of their adventure, the next step in a day full of unexpected events.

Their enjoyment segues into confusion as they're plunged into darkness. The boat gathers speed and the disorientated and queasy passengers become more and more agitated as grotesque, disjointed images flash on the walls of the tunnel while the boat hurtles forward into the darkness.

They plead with him to stop, but Gene Wilder's Wonka becomes alive with the thrill of the chaos. The tension builds to panic, and as a child watching, I became just as unsettled as the characters, wanting to return to the colour, candy and comfort of the 'world of pure imagination'.

With a chaotic crescendo, the boat stops. The lights come up and it's almost equally shocking to see everything is the exact same, the horror of the tunnel disappearing as unexpectedly as it appeared.

Many nights I've been in that tunnel, stepped on board cautiously. Seeking reassurance but allowing myself to be carried along by the journey. Then it all changed, trips down memory lane, safe, enjoyable memories disintegrated and morphed into events both real and imagined. My fears projected onto a screen in front of me in the darkness. The sound so deafening, that I couldn't help but listen to words taunt and mock me. I was scared, disorientated, it felt so real, like I had no control over how fast I was going or the images and thoughts I was being assaulted with.

Mr Wonka, I want to get off!

A lot of the nights I gave in, I believed. Tears came hard and fast, lugging despair with them. Sobs travelled from what felt like the centre of my being and I doubled over, not sure whether the pain was emotional or physical at this stage. It felt hopeless. *I'm a horrible person and I need to make it up to people. I need to prove that I'm worthy of their friendship, their attention and affection. Their love.*

Some nights I gritted my teeth and rode it out like a monstrous rollercoaster, clenching my gut against the gnarled twists and drops. Morning would bring a respite, I was sure … ish.

Other times, waking was as if in slow motion. My alarm would ring:

Snooze. Alarm. Snooze. Alarm … *I'm going to be late, really late. But I can't open my eyes.* Glued shut with groggy sleep, I already knew it was there. I knew how I felt before I'd even started the scramble to make up for the time I'd lost hitting the snooze button. My muscles ached and there was a weighted feeling in my chest, in my whole body. The tears had already started. They had their own schedule and agenda, just doing their own thing, irrespective of the situation, of the growing list of things to do in the shortening space of time. I only noticed them when they dropped onto the lap of my pyjamas. With a heavy sigh, I would begin the tussle between calling in sick or starting to get ready. I'd like to say that most of the time I chose to get up, to put one foot in front of the other and slowly start to assemble a presentable version of myself ... but I'd be lying.

The warm refuge of the duvet won many, many times. Even years later that sentence affects me like the sound of nails on a blackboard, has me sucking in air through my teeth. I couldn't shake the notion of being lazy, of letting people down, not being able to 'brave face' it. I just couldn't. It wasn't so much about not wanting people to see me like that (I didn't) but more that I wanted to spare people from being around me. To use far kinder language than I would have at the time, I wasn't the best version of myself. I'd give myself a day in bed, I'd recharge and I'd do better tomorrow.

On those 'tomorrows' I would operate in slow motion, dazed, shell-shocked, out of it. (Sometimes I was. I remember having a dosage of an antidepressant that I had to split between morning and evening. In the clunky clamber to get out the door in the morning, I swallowed the two tablets by accident. It wasn't until I'd reached work that I realised something was wrong. I copped my mistake and rang my doctor. Not ideal but

I was in no imminent danger. I'd just be drowsy for a few hours. I fabricated a, no doubt, feeble excuse and had to be driven home. My gratefulness at being back in the safety and privacy of my bed only lasted until I realised I'd have to explain to my then boyfriend what had happened, explain that it *was* an accident, and deal with his inevitable disgust.)

I was so embarrassed, so ashamed. This was a time where social media was Myspace and the beginnings of Facebook. Thankfully I didn't have to subject myself to the endless toxic platitudes of *positive vibes only.* But I knew what I brought to the party. I knew I wasn't a fun person to be around. My words would spill out and I'd let slip hints at the negative distortion of thoughts inside. I wished I was different. Processing instructions or even innocuous greetings was an arduous task. I'd scan them for criticism or hints that they could see what was going on. I thought everyone could see it, could smell it off me, as if I'd been branded with a giant 'Depressed' across the back of my shoulders that let people know how weak and inept I was.

In 2020, when Caroline Flack was found to have died by suicide, social media responded and rallied with messages of 'be kind'.

In a world where you can be anything, be kind.

Words of encouragement: talk to someone, have empathy and, most of all, be kind.

I remember scrolling through my feed on Instagram. People sympathised and thanked God that they themselves didn't have mental health issues, that they were positive, strong people.

I stared at my screen. The sides of my vision went fuzzy and my mouth dried up.

I understood the intention: words are important, they hold weight. If 'positive and strong' is held up as the opposite of having 'mental health issues', what does that make me or anyone else whose eyes shoot open, unexplained, at 4.48 a.m. each morning?

Negative and weak.

Back then it was my biggest fear. Not just that that's how people perceived me, but that that's who I was, what I was.

Negative and weak.

Living your life trying to prove to others, to yourself, that you are *not* is like having a thirst that, no matter how many glasses of water you pour down your neck, won't be quenched. It's relentless, rife with misunderstood intentions, polarising and, most of all, exhausting.

My time was spent denying, compensating or apologising. Not out loud or in my actions but, most of the time, in my head. It was a noisy place filled with arguments, rebuttals, push-back, anger and a feeling of being misunderstood. If I could just prove myself to them … It was my full-time job, and I worked around it. It was a game of life-or-death importance and I played with steely determination. I would not get caught. The barrage of symptoms nipped at my heels, tripped me up, and still, I kept stumbling forward.

Of course I fell, I lost the game. Maybe I was just too tired, but in 2008, having just turned 26, I got caught.

You're It!

Fine, I surrender.

Now what?

A cycle of medications, meetings with doctors and hospital admissions followed. So did anger, so much anger. Diagnoses were made and then changed. Depression, yup, that made sense. Bipolar disorder? Okay, that sounded more impressive, more legitimate. Plus, the women on the ward who had bipolar disorder seemed to have way more fun than the rest of us. They largely congregated in the smoking room while we sat in front of the television, knitting. I'd sometimes peer into the room through the plumes of smoke when I was getting my evening cup of tea from the trolley. It looked so much more ... energetic than where I spent my evenings.

At least I had a name for it now. To paraphrase my doctor at the time, 'that which we call a rose, by any other name, would smell as shit'. Maybe the name wasn't all that important. Recognising the triggers, the symptoms and how to manage them was what mattered.

Years later, that diagnosis was changed to borderline personality disorder. I've barely ever said that aloud, let alone committed it to paper. This one I couldn't get on board with at all. I had switched from private care to the public mental health system. I was diagnosed by a doctor who had not previously met me, but made his assessment based on the findings of his registrar. I was unable to speak as I listened to him recount information that was incorrect, nuances missed. Tears fell heavily into my lap as I felt helpless, unable to advocate for myself and like I was falling between the cracks.

So I skipped the J1 visa, interrailing, the year in Australia, typical pilgrimages people my age were doing. The *road to recovery* was the only travelling I did. I don't know if you've been on that road but this was a time before smartphones and Google Maps and boy, let me tell you, it's easy to get lost. You'd think it'd be straightforward:

Just stay on the road.

What they don't tell you is that sometimes the road forks and you don't know which is the best route, *or* other times the road is like a motorway that you're driving, the route stretching ahead of you for miles, monotonous and boring miles ... so you pop on the indicator and take a detour through a town just for a change of scenery. I spent most of my 20s and early 30s on that road. I'd got lost so many times, I felt I couldn't ask for directions any more.

I needed to breathe. Not the short, shallow breaths that keep you alive, ticking over but locked into a state of fight or flight, merely existing. I wanted that breath that starts deep down in your being and fills your lungs and limbs with life, opens your eyes to the colours, your nose to the smells and your ears to the sounds, that breath that meets fear and discomfort with a calm certainty that this will pass. Without knowing it, I wanted that breath that places you in the world, lungs open, heart open: living, a part of it.

New Year's Eve, 2014, I booked a plane ticket.

I'd fly into Panama City and home from Lima, Peru, two months later. Where I went and what I did in between that was wide open; the thought was exhilarating.

I booked a hostel for the first night and after that I'd play it by ear. Of course, the first morning in the hostel I met a lad from Cahersiveen. He had teamed up with a lad from Waterford and they were going to get a boat from Panama to Colombia via the San Blas islands in a few days' time. Did I fancy joining them? That was the first shrug of my shoulders accompanied by a scared–excited 'sure', allowing my path to be shaped by the people I met and opportunities that presented themselves.

That boat trip mimicked an episode of *Fawlty Towers*. The captain was a mercurial Argentinian who seemed to resent having *gringos* on his boat. Deliberately or accidentally, they had overbooked the voyage, so with two fewer sleeping spaces than was required, we were packed in tightly. Strangers were put together in small double beds. Early in the trip, I escaped the heat of my tiny bed and cabin that I shared with a delightful, statuesque German girl. Climbing up on deck, I settled into a makeshift hammock. The sky was black, and with the horizon indecipherable in the darkness, it seemed to loop under me, cradling the boat among the stars with their twinkling reflections. The vastness of it all struck me. Here I was, a tiny dot, miles from home. I felt so grateful to be there, in that moment. The possibilities of the trip stretched out before me. I felt giddy but more settled than I had in a long while. I felt free.

A few days into the boat trip, we got caught in a storm. Ashen-faced, people hung their heads over the side, browbeaten by sea sickness. I lived on a diet of Ritz crackers and travel sickness tablets and, though I have a history of getting queasy on boats, I seemed to escape the worst of it. We were days longer at sea than was planned and ran out of food. When we were dropped off a couple of hundred miles from where was intended, we were all a little bit green and stinking, but a fairly bonded group. The eclectic mix of personalities had gelled in this crazy experience and there was nothing left to do but laugh and grab snacks and beers as the Spanish speakers among us deputised and arranged for transport that would finally take us to Cartagena.

This group was my travelling family for the first two weeks of my trip. There was safety in numbers and unending craic in their company. Saying goodbye to them as we all went our separate ways was difficult, an initiation into the ritual of intense travelling friendships and the inevitable goodbyes.

I spent the next few months *not* saying 'no'. It started off as a way to make sure I didn't waste my trip by staying in my comfort zone, by *not* starting up conversations with strangers, by saying 'no' to something just because I didn't think it was my thing. Instead I said yes, sometimes tentatively, sometimes emphatically but always curiously. Yes. Yes to new adventures, new activities and new opportunities. I kept a few 'no' cards in my back pocket for situations where safety called for them, but I used them sparingly.

Who do you think you are?

What will people think?

What if it all goes wrong?

You shouldn't be doing this.

This isn't the right way to do things.

I don't know if they didn't have valid passports or just couldn't get the time off work, but these usual companions didn't seem to have made the journey with me. It felt quieter without them but decision-making suddenly became a lot easier. No stalling, doubting, reconsidering. Better yet, those decisions were followed by actions. There's little time to over-analyse when the overnight bus leaves in an hour and you have to navigate your way to the station with your non-existent Spanish.

Why had I not done this sooner? Letting go of 'at-home Claire' was so liberating. I didn't undergo a full personality transformation but it felt, for the first time, that I was giving myself a break. Something I *should* have been doing a long time ago. Stepping outside my head and just giving it a go.

I made and said goodbye to new friends every couple of days. I took chances; I made spontaneous decisions that saw me running to buses to destinations I'd only learned of hours beforehand. I spoke to people. Not that that's difficult when staying in hostels – people there are open to meeting others. But I initiated conversations without trying to be someone I was not. To my delight I found that people gravitated towards me, seemed to like having me around. It was thrilling to move about and interact as this lighter version of myself.

I did my scuba certification, and though I felt a little bit panicky underwater, like reverse vertigo, (don't look *up*!), I was enthralled by the scenes, the weightlessness, the simple learning of a new skill. I was seeing everything in full colour, soaking up each new experience and feeling a sense of openness and possibility that had been absent for quite a while. I was living.

I let my curiosity lead me.

'How did you learn how to do that? Is it dangerous? Can anyone do it?'

'What's the name of the place again?'

'How far is it from here, do you reckon?'

'There's a ferry in two days – do you think I can make it in time?'

And that's the series of questions that led me to the island of Utila. Bikini instead of bra, flip-flops tucked into the side of my rucksack, barefoot I walked into the school.

'Beginners freediving course starts tomorrow at 2 p.m.,' I was informed.

As I scribbled my name across application forms and waivers, the squiggle of little footprints across the map of my travels, criss-crossing South and Central America, there was a lightness, a return of divilment, a spark that had been dulled in the comfortable grounds of home.

This sport was about to show me a new way of living. Breathing fully, being present are just the tip of the iceberg. I was about to see a full world *between* the inhale and exhale, where I would learn to trust myself, be kinder to myself, to celebrate my strength and embrace my softness. Freediving would facilitate and provide a way for me to come back to myself, again and again.

I was capable of so much more than I had ever believed …

And it was all about to begin.

chapter 2

WIDTHS, WAVES AND WASHING MACHINES

I grew up in Kildare, a landlocked county in Ireland more known for its racecourses than roaring waves. Yet the sea feels like it was a part of my childhood. Summer holidays to Irish seasides, squinting, trying to make out the colour of the flag in the distance. 'Yellow and red, yellow and red, yellow and red,' we'd repeat, fingers crossed in anticipation. A red flag was a no-swim day. You'd be stuck making poxy sandcastles if that was the case. The Judy Blume that was tucked away in my new 'going on holidays' bag might spare me from that fate, but with three younger siblings, you'd never know. 'YELLOW! It's yellow and red!' Fists closed and that triumphant jerk of my elbow towards my side would accompany the extra sibilant '*Yessssssss*'. There was a lifeguard on duty. We were in business.

Bursting out of the car once it came to a stop, stripping down to my togs on the run to the beach (I'd put them on beforehand – this wasn't my first rodeo). Being grabbed for the cursory blob of sun cream to be lashed onto my shoulders and face. It was overcast and 17 degrees. The only fair-skinned and freckled child among my sallow-skinned siblings, I'd somehow manage to be raw red within an hour. Better leg it before Mum suggested I wear a T-shirt over my togs.

'Go and get a good stone for the windbreaker.' No swim before set-up, those were the rules. We all knew exactly what type of stone to search for. Windbreakers were a key piece of equipment on the beach in the early 90s. Ninety per cent of the families around us had the same blue windbreaker with the stripe of rainbow colours two-thirds of the way down.

Blankets laid, I'd skirt the perimeter to dump the pile of jumpers I was allocated to carry. You didn't *dare* walk across the blanket with sandy feet. Buckets and spades were flung down unceremoniously, and the cooler and picnic bag were delivered with care to the prime spot, beside Mum and sheltered from the wind. Mum settled herself, removing her fleece. She was as determined to sunbathe as we were to hit the water.

'Do you want to come for a swim, Mum?' We both knew the answer but tradition was tradition.

'I'll stay here and mind the bags.' I never understood how she could resist the splashing and messing, but Mum wasn't a swimmer. Not only that, she hated the water. I knew the story. My granny paid for Mum to have swimming lessons. As one of nine children, this was a big deal. Mum hid during the lessons, wetting her hair in the shower before she went home. It's always weird to think of your parents as children but this was even stranger. It was like reading about a bold character in a book rather than being able to attribute this as an action by my own mum! 'Did Granny not kill you?' I must have exclaimed a hundred times. I don't know if my granny ever found out or her reaction, but to this day, my mum doesn't know how to swim.

'Wait for Dad!' followed us on the wind as our little legs pegged it down to the shore. The tide was out and I relished the feeling of the sand changing from dry powdered sugar to wet and squelchy between my toes. I wasn't much of an athletic child, but for this, I'd run. Dad, not far behind us, would arrive and splash us if we took too long to get in. It wasn't worth the risk. I'd wade in further and further, going up onto my tiptoes as waves came and splashed higher up onto my red swimsuit, my breath catching in my throat. The theatrics of getting in were in full swing behind me. Dad was running in, screaming and running back out, letting the waves *almost* catch him. My brother Matt, still a baby, watched, trying to escape Mum's hold, already eager to get involved. My sisters looked on, squealing in delight. 'Come on!' Katie shouted impatiently at Dad. White-blonde hair tied up in a Leixlip plait (Mum's version of a French plait) and with a fringe that started halfway back on her head, Katie was making her way out to me. Back arched and childish belly sticking out, she looked as she often did: determined. Sarah stood on the shore, skinny and already shivering. Dad scooped her up and brought her in, accompanied by much protesting. She'd be dumped in the water fairly shortly. Rookie mistake.

I don't remember swimming as much as playing. Hours in the water, getting knocked over by waves, handstand competitions, seaweed fights or simply looking up at the sky, floating on my back. Emerging with wrinkly fingers, our hair plastered to our skulls and sand lining the inside of our swimsuits, we'd return to the picnic blanket to devour ham sandwiches with crisps on the side. Sandwiches never tasted as good, the white bread sticking to the roof of my mouth and bits of sand grinding between my teeth. And the crisps? Well, a picnic wasn't a picnic if you didn't have crisps.

Different beaches, different years; a slideshow of Irish summers as a child. Swimming in the rain, the clouds and the lucky blue-sky days, I remember so many images ... but I don't remember the cold. I remember the giddy delight of peeling my socks off and plunging my feet into the warm(ish) sand for the first time that year. I remember the smell of coconut sun cream and seaweed that, to this day, reminds me of the Irish beaches of home. I remember making sandcastles dressed in jumpers and windcheaters. But I never remember being cold. It was summer. The sea air might increase your appetite and the salt water do funny things to your hair, but in those hours wading through the sea, feeling the resistance against your legs or the weightless feeling of floating on your back, limbs bobbing on the surface, neither time nor temperature mattered.

Actual swimming was done in the pool: Saturday mornings and then Saturday evenings and, over the years, a Tuesday and a Thursday thrown in here and there for good measure. I went through togs quicker than I could move through water. I have an incredible gift, passed down from my dad's side, of forgetting or losing things. 'I definitely put them in my bag. I remember!' I swore blindly. But each trip to the chlorine-smelling Lost Property would reveal my still soggy swimsuit.

Saturday evenings were Sportsco swims. These were where it all started, where I learned to swim and maybe just as importantly, where I learned to play. These lessons were the foundation, with the other midweek sessions or training added over the years.

The very first session, I came out of the women's changing room and was greeted by the swimming teacher, Pat.

'How old are you?'

My small, wide feet on the beige tiles below me is an image I can still see as clearly as a photograph as I answered, 'Seven.'

'Aren't you a tall girl for seven?'

And that is my memory of the first Saturday-night session that would continue to be a weekend staple for the next 10 years.

You started in the 'widths' group – no cute tadpole/frog/dolphin group names for us wannabe swimmers in the 80s. Widths or lengths, you were either with Pat or Kevin.

Widths: I remember a lot of kicking. Mostly in the water, sometimes at Katie if she went over onto my side. With the board, on our backs, our legs kicked furiously with maximum splashing as we moved at a snail's pace through the water. The more splashes the better.

'Tuck your chin in. Don't look at the ceiling – look back at me.'

I didn't like the backstroke much. But I knew we'd have one more go of blowing bubbles holding onto the bar before we finished up, so it was fine.

Once you had blown your quota of bubbles and wiggled over and back the width of the pool with relative competency, you progressed to lengths: the big leagues. That's where most of my memories are, ploughing up and down the pool in a crooked line. Dad would swim his quota of lengths in the lane beside us and, as I progressed, I'd try to time it so that I'd be swimming beside him, measuring my speed against his, all the while checking the clock and willing it to 6.45 p.m. Once the clock turned 6.45 p.m., lessons were over and it was playtime.

Playtime always kicked off with races. I'd get a five-second head start from Dad, Katie would get a five-second head start from me and Sarah five seconds from Katie. We'd thrash up the pool leaving nothing behind. As our hands hit the wall, red faced and puffing we'd lift our heads to see if we'd won.

Some might think that a father would let his daughter win. Not in our family. We were all competitive and we had to get it from somewhere. If I won, I'd earned the win – a messy, thrashy, goggles-around-the-neck win was still a win. We loved it.

We'd break out the handstands on the rare occasions Mum came to watch. Calling for her, trying to get her attention as she spoke to other observing mums enduring the stuffy heat. 'MUM! Did you see? I just did a really good one' – if I had stayed up for a full 10 seconds and my toes had been extra pointy. Mum would wave and return to her conversation, and I, unsure if she'd caught it, would repeat the display, just in case. We'd play chasing and dive for rings in the deep end of the pool, ears popping the whole way.

The way home was just as much part of it as the swim. Piling into the car, our wet hair making dark puddles on the backs of our jumpers, Dad would blast the heat so the car acted as a communal hairdryer. Our journey home was passed with a weekly quiz that we'd beg him to start once we'd buckled our seatbelts. We'd arrive home 25 minutes later, cheeks bright red and hair expanding in all its frizzy glory.

Rinse. Repeat.

Every single Saturday.

They're happy memories, all melded together, from when I was seven up until seventeen. At the time, I never associated them with a love of water. It was just something I did, *we* did, as a family. Water was to be respected but ultimately was for exploring and playing in. I presumed that's how everyone felt.

♦ ♦ ♦

I left Ireland at the start of February 2015 and started to make my way down through Colombia and into Ecuador, taking in as many coastal towns and islands as I could. Shortly before leaving Colombia, I met a guy. Yup, my first real holiday romance since meeting a blond Welsh lad on a Keycamp holiday in France when I was 12. Unlike the Welsh boy (who wrote to me for the rest of that summer), I fell for this one. Hard. We shared glasses of rum under canopies of palm trees in the Cocora valley and passed joints back and forth under glittering starry skies. We filled each other in on the significant events in our lives in that rush to connect that saw us finishing each other's sentences. I got the impression I wasn't the only one breathing a sigh of relief at being able to leave aspects of myself or life behind at home.

All too soon, as is the way with holiday flings, we said our goodbyes. I wish I could say I played it cool and shrugged with the indifferent cynicism of someone who knows better. But this 32-year-old woman had had horrible luck with men in the previous few years, had confused 'putting herself out there' with tolerating subpar 'well, at least you'll have great stories' behaviour. Her confidence with men (or maybe her confidence full stop) had been chipped away bit by bit, date by date, and rebuffed with the reliable Irish tools of self-deprecation and humour. She – *I* – just wanted to be loved. I didn't think that he was *the one* and that I'd move to England and be a geography teacher's wife. But it didn't stop the fantasy and it had opened up a yearning that I'd tried so hard to deny and brush off. Those wonderful, magical few days in a bubble of a holiday fling brought home something that I was desperately trying to disprove: I wanted someone to share adventures with, and most of all, I wanted to love and be loved.

And that's how I found myself in Quito. Hungover, lovesick for this poor unknowing guy and, despite this exotic adventure, feeling as grey as the weather, I made the decision to fly to the Galapagos on a whim.

The Galapagos hadn't been on my travel plan. I'd heard it was expensive and my deal with myself was that I would not come back from this trip broke. That was going quickly out the window as I sat googling flights in the hostel computer room. Having hastily filled in my passport number and hit *purchase now*, I headed back up to my dorm to pack my stuff. I was getting out of here and, like many of my decisions this trip, I was doing it now.

Since setting out from Ireland, I had done my PADI scuba certification. I had gone white-water rafting; I'd snorkelled and swam and abseiled down waterfalls. Apart from a brief and never-to-be-repeated foray into paragliding, the majority of my activities revolved around water. There's an unofficial trail that backpackers were following and you'd often hear recommendations along the way. I made sure to challenge myself, to push myself out of my comfort zone and say yes to things I normally wouldn't (please see aforementioned paragliding), but in the Galapagos, I just wanted to be in the water. At the time, I didn't make a connection between heartbreak and fleeing to be by the sea. At home, I'd often find myself parked near Sandycove. Whether the waves were lapping gently or crashing wildly, they always soothed whatever unrest had caused me to grab my keys and jump into my car. Difficult decisions, disappointing dates or emotions that often felt too big for my body were processed beside the sea. Whether I was walking alongside it, floating in it or even watching the water from my car, I knew that when I felt off-kilter it was a place I could go to regain my sense of equilibrium. My heart was aching a little, and at the time I didn't care what I did in the water: scuba, swim, surf or snorkel, I just wanted to be in it, on it or under it. Full immersion.

On my very first excursion, a snorkelling trip to a popular dive spot, the boat was joined by a pod of dolphins. Thirty to forty of them swam alongside the bow, playing, splashing and causing people to trip over themselves as they scurried for cameras. For once, I didn't reach for my phone. I sat on the floor and slipped my legs underneath the bar, letting them dangle over the side. I couldn't believe what I was seeing – I needed a moment to take it in.

The captain decided to make an impromptu stop. Anyone who wanted to could get in the water. I was already hooking my bikini with one hand and pulling up my pants with the other. 'Anyone who is a strong swimmer and confident in the water go to the back of the boat and you'll be helped in.'

I know my limitations and I know my abilities and I sent out a silent 'thank you, thank you, thank you' to Mum and Dad as I jumped in the water. Though Mum didn't swim, my parents had encouraged our appreciation of water, drove us to endless swimming lessons, normalised being in the sea, and Dad nurtured not only a love of the water, but how to approach it with playfulness. Being knocked by waves was a game, you remained calm and went with the tumble, softening your body until you could stand up. We experienced fear, but instead of it stopping us, Dad had helped us channel it into respect. In the water, we were comfortable, confident but never complacent. So as a 32-year-old woman I could jump off the boat, head submerging to be greeted by the sound of 30 dolphin whistles. I tried to catch my breath through my snorkel as the strong, athletic grey bodies undulated in front of me, all my senses tingling with fear and delight. It was a rare occasion where you realise the magic of what is surely a once-off experience and every part of you is consumed by taking in every possible detail and sensation.

Out of the corner of my eye, I spotted another shape, moving differently, circling the perimeter. Was that a …? I exhaled and held my breath, allowing my body to sink below the surface to take another look. It was! A shark! I couldn't believe it. We'd been told about the different species of shark indigenous to the Galapagos Islands. This was my very first time seeing one. We were assured they were not dangerous, but years of films and the chilling *Jaws* theme had my heart beating in my throat. It was terrifying and exhilarating. The few of us who had got in the water climbed out a short while later, elated, with animated high fives flying in all directions to bridge the language barriers.

Without a doubt a once-in-a-lifetime file for the memory shelf, and I couldn't have been more grateful.

I was here. I was doing it. I was alive!

My time in the Galapagos was indeed a trip of a lifetime. Seven years later, it has that clichéd fog surrounding it, almost dreamlike. The warm hue of rose-tinted glasses. Did it really happen? It did. I had the folder of photos on my old laptop as proof. So much of my time there was spent, not exploring the island, the source of inspiration for Darwin's theory of evolution, but underwater. With each boat ride, I'd get a shiver of anticipation, the sheer excitement of looking out to dark blue meeting light blue, with the occasional blue-footed booby breaking things up, of knowing that once your head dipped below the water, a new world, a new experience, would reveal itself. New colours, new conditions, new currents and, oh, more marine life than I'd ever dreamt of seeing. I was testing my newly acquired advanced scuba certification to the max but the promise of seeing hammerhead sharks was too enticing. Home and the events of the last few years, the packing up of apartments, the shitty first dates on wintery Tuesday evenings, the tail lights and condensation-fogged windows of rush-hour traffic on the M50, they all felt very far away. But most of all, I felt ... unshackled? I didn't seem to have the same litany of protests, of self-doubt each time it came to making a decision. I was so immersed in doing, in being, rooted in the sensory, I was soaking up the experiences. Maybe the very prospect of seeing a shark forces you out of your head and into your body, the visceral reaction not leaving much space for spiralling introspection! Each time we zipped up our wetsuits, clipped on our buoyancy devices, or BCDs, we willed them into the waters below us as we practised bumping our closed fist to the side of our head, the underwater sign for hammerhead shark.

At Gordon's Rock, hammerheads were *almost* a guarantee. We had briefed the dive – the word 'washing machine' was thrown out describing the currents. Gordon's Rock is a volcano crater with three pinnacles that rise above the surface, its silhouette synonymous with diving in the Galapagos. It was not for beginners but my nervousness was laced with excitement. I couldn't wait to get in the water.

I am embarrassed to say, dear reader, that I was the weakest link on this dive. We were briefed that once one person hit 100 bar on their oxygen tank, we'd all head back to the boat, do the safety stop and resurface together. It was me: I was that person. I had been pretty good with my air consumption, but on this dive, I couldn't help myself. It turns out shrieks underwater use a considerable amount of air. It's not something I'd done much of before, but if ever there was a dive that called for it, this was it: lying sideways, flat against the rock that stretched towards the surface and beyond, fingers clutching onto the smallest of ridges and turning my face away from the current because the sheer force hit the purge button on my regulator. Dark and shadowed water, I looked up for light to see 20 hammerhead sharks silhouetted against the surface overhead. I was giddy – and scared shitless. I wasn't thinking about what I was doing later on, what I'd got up to yesterday, the call home I still had to return or the impending flights I wanted to push out – again. I wanted to be nowhere else but there, underwater.

And that was it: the ocean was a place to explore, to play, to revel in the warm, clear water when away, and to brace yourself against and brave it out when at home.

A place for adventure, flow and fun ...

Until freediving.

chapter 3

BEGINNINGS OF BREATHHOLD

I can't remember when I was first introduced to what I now know to be freediving. Different memories stand out but at the time, I didn't know what I was seeing. I didn't know it had a name, was an actual sport or the extent of what was possible. I just know that I was struck by how impressive and beautiful it was in equal measure.

I know all those Saturday evenings in Sportsco introduced me to the idea of holding my breath, diving down from the surface, even if it was just in the deep end of a pool. Whether to simply touch the bottom or scurry across the tiled floor collecting rings, it was a regular playtime activity.

I grew up knowing how to handle myself in water, to be a confident swimmer, to have respect for the sea and, when it came to open water, to play by the rules. Water informed my travel, my downtime and even my creative work. But freediving? Until 2015, I'd never heard of it.

During my time in the Galapagos, scuba dives were interspersed with snorkel trips. Not just off-the-shore snorkel trips but day trips to different sites, stopping along the way for swims, snorkels, photos and food.

On one particular excursion, we'd enjoyed a morning with penguins, huge turtles and the most playful seals I'd ever encountered. Around lunchtime, the crew dropped the anchor and I grabbed the plastic flippers they provided, along with a snorkel and mask. One of the crew members joined me and we splashed about in the water as we waited for lunch.

Face in the water, I looked at all the colours of the fish that swam mere metres from my face. My buddy splashed beside me, folding at the waist, hand on his nose, his small fins propelling him down. Further and further from the surface, his outline softened and his movements blended in with the marine life around him. I was no longer looking at the fish. Growing up on the nearby island, it was clear that this water had been his playground. It was like he was one of them. *This is the closest thing to a merman I'm going to see*, I thought, in awe. I'd only recently learned words like buoyancy, and how to control it with air in your BCD, but this guy … though he was in possession of only the most rudimentary equipment, nothing looked like it was an issue. His axis tilted and he swam head down, toes towards the surface, grabbing hold of a rock below him and pulling himself down to play peekaboo with the reef sharks resting underneath. He was brave, he was free, at ease, his movements appeared effortless and it was, by far, the most beautiful and impressive thing I had seen on this trip.

This Galapagueño merman was the first time I was struck by the beauty of freediving – I just didn't know it yet.

A few months later, I was in Belize – Belize! I type it so casually but years later I still shiver at how exotic it sounds. I was there! At the time I didn't take it for granted – I knew it was a privilege to be there, a once-in-a-life-time experience.

It was another boat trip, another snorkelling excursion. It's all I wanted to do. I'd concede a trip inland for exploration of mountains, volcanoes and waterfalls if it could be bookended by trips to the coast – or better yet, a small island.

I set out to explore the reef with a group of Aussie lads I'd met that morning. Confident and competent in the water, as most Australian backpackers I'd encountered were, they kicked down, disappearing to explore a cave and to emerge (what felt like) minutes later on the other side. Without realising, I'd been holding my breath just watching. I jerked my head out of the water and pulled my mask from my eyes, taking big breaths and letting the air hit my face.

How the hell can they do that?

I wanted to keep up. I considered myself relatively proficient in the water and more than a little bit competitive, so I decided I'd follow them and keep up.

I knew about equalising from scuba-diving. Equalising is matching the pressure in the airspace of your middle ear with the external pressure surrounding you. Descending from the surface, divers have to learn techniques to push air from the lungs into the middle ear to balance the pressure change. I'd just carry over the skill and swim to them as quickly as I could, minimising the time I had to hold my breath. Thankfully my ears stopped me before my breathhold did. Only a few metres from the surface I came to a screeching halt as my ears were hit by pressure and pain. It was much easier when there was a tank of air on your back and you'd an endless supply to push into your ears.

There must be a knack to it, I thought. *But how do they know how to do it?*

We clinked cheers and sipped bottles of beer on our sail back to shore. I'd never get fed up with these sunsets or the tight feeling of my skin from a mixture of sun and salt water.

'So how did you guys learn how to do that?' I asked, trying but landing nowhere near close to blasé.

'Oh, that's called freediving. We did some courses in it last month.'

'Freediving? Cool.'

I moved to another subject, all the while repeating,

freedivingfreedivingfreediving, don't forget the name.

Later that evening, I'd showered and then showered in mosquito spray and declined the invitation to drinks after dinner. I pulled out my phone and wandered to different spots in the hostel, my arm outstretched until the Wi-Fi signal suddenly brought my phone to life with pings and notifications.

Where can you learn freediving?

Do you mean cliff diving?

No, I did not! Shit, had I spelt it wrong?

Freediving + Central America

Freediving Utila: Central America's first freediving school in the Caribbean. Learn to hold your breath and go deeper than you ever thought.

Where is Utila?

Utila (Isla de Utila) is the smallest of Honduras's major Bay Islands.

How do you get from Caye Caulker, Belize to Utila ...?

I won't pretend that I felt any pull of fate or the universe redirecting me or something more divine than my own sense of curiosity and perhaps competitiveness. This whole trip, I'd travelled changing plans on a whim, mapping out routes based on activities I'd heard about, seen or that had come recommended. Sometimes I'd travelled to spots I'd little interest in because I'd joined up with an interesting travel companion and she was on her way there. The experience was just as much about the people as it was the places or activities. Freediving had piqued my interest like scuba-diving had, like zip lining had, like white-water rafting had. I'd give it a go and see what direction it took me in.

And that's how and why I landed on Utila, padding barefoot up the main street and veering into the shop with the *21 metres on one breath* sign outside.

I planned to stay for two weeks, splitting my time between freediving and scuba-diving. I stayed for the remaining four weeks of my trip, rerouting my flights to Ireland out from San Pedro Sula on the mainland … and I never put a tank of air on my back again.

♦ ♦ ♦

Freediving is, in essence, holding your breath and travelling underwater. Whether used to explore a coral reef or marine life, or attached to a line and seeing how deep you can go all on one breath, freediving is a recreational as well as a competitive sport.

Freediving is NOT:

- Jumping from a cliff into water
- Going down and taking air at depth from a scuba tank before coming back up (my phone-typing accustomed fingers are searching for the horrified face emoji to insert here)

And it is also NOT:

- *Not* having to pay for your scuba dives.

These are probably the three most common misconceptions of freediving I've experienced.

Divided into different disciplines, it's measured in time, distance or depth. Let's start with the pool disciplines: These cover the time and distances elements.

First up we have the dynamic and dynamic no fins disciplines.

Think back to when you were younger, messing and splashing about in the pool. Now, tell the truth, did you or did you not try to swim the length of the pool underwater? I did. I still see adults finishing off their 'weekly laps' by the playtime activity of trying to swim to the opposite end on one breath.

This is a crude introduction to pool freediving!

There are different ways to propel yourself through the water. The method will often (but not always) determine how far you go. The first way is with long fins, or bi-fins. We're familiar with the scissor-like kick used in front crawl. The fins method uses a similar kick, just far slower, wearing fins on your feet.

From bi-fins we go to monofin. This time both feet are in a single fin, which requires a dolphin kick. When the diver has good technique and flexibility, it can look like the lower part of their body is undulating independent from the upper part, the fluidity making it look like the bones below the bottom of their ribcage have melted to form a powerful and graceful tail.

Some prefer to leave the fins off altogether. No fins is a discipline that combines a similar kick to a breast stroke, with arms that trace a keyhole stroke. Under their own power, no-fin divers are always impressive in their ability to balance power, energy and efficiency.

Next up we have static apnea, which describes perfectly what it is: lying still, or static, and holding your breath for as long as you can. Done in the pool, this typically will be your longest breathhold.

Maybe it's not the most exciting of spectator sports, but I find it fascinating to observe. Okay, you're watching someone face down, airways submerged in water, their coach maybe whispering reminders or applying pressure to parts of their back that push them into the water to pop up again, limbs floppy and relaxed. Some athletes don't like to be touched at all. But it is incredible to watch the stopwatch clock up five, six, seven-plus minutes with the athlete barely moving other than responding to the occasional 'give me an okay' instruction.

Doing static is challenging. There is no movement, no lovely deep blue waters to distract and take your mind away from the discomfort and challenge. Maybe that's why, in my humble freediving opinion, it's the purest discipline. Or if not the purest, the most fundamental aspect of freediving: holding your breath in water.

Face down, legs and arms floating, it's just you, your body, your breath and your mind. That's it. Thinking about the everyday distractions that pull on our attention throughout the day, it may seem like bliss. *Peace and quiet at last – I'd love a bit of static apnea*, you might think as your phone buzzes with email alerts and text messages, a car beeps its horn behind you and the clock ticks past your anticipated arrival time.

How often do we simply sit with our own thoughts, with no music on, no phones in our hands to distract us, and just be? Not only that, how often do we sit with our thoughts and observe them, distance ourselves from them, decline the sometimes-forceful invitation they issue to follow them down a rabbit hole, descending in a spiral beyond our field of vision? Not often. Those thoughts, the things that are responsible for the stress we don't even realise we hold in our body, the clenching of our teeth, the furrowing of our brows, the shoulders that have encroached upon the space previously held by a lengthened neck. Thoughts of deadlines, plans, worries, strategies, to-do lists, stresses that keep you awake at night, your body vibrating with tension when your eyes beg for sleep.

There are few places that force me into the present moment like static apnea. Here, I question all previous notions of relaxation. Here, I learn to observe my thoughts, not judge them, not attach a story or meaning but simply observe and let them float past my eyes. The same thing with sensations: reactions are postponed or maybe even facilitated. There's a softness to it, a detachment from the discomfort, the mind being in the driving seat and beckoning you forward, promising something *just on the other side*.

It is an exercise in mindfulness like nothing I've experienced before. To be in just that moment, and then the next, and then the next. It is somewhere I've learned a different definition of strong and, always surprisingly, the softness it takes to get there. In times when my monkey mind is swinging out of branches and throwing shit against the walls inside my head, I know putting my face in the water will bring me on a breathhold journey that will indicate how I'm doing, what I need to work on and bring me right down out of my head and into my body, my attention nowhere else but in *just this moment*.

Anyone who mentions that they freedive will almost certainly be asked, 'How long can you hold your breath?'

To the uninitiated, the length of your breath is the distinguishing feature of freedivers, the measure of your ability.

It's not. Without a doubt, telling people you can hold your breath for 5 minutes and 59 seconds is a useful icebreaker. Then you follow it up by telling them that's roughly the length of 'Bohemian Rhapsody' and they speed hum the different sections finishing with a 'Nothing really matters to me' gasp of disbelief. But while each pool discipline is respected and can showcase beyond-human skills, I know 100-metre divers who seldom train and can't remember their static record. For them, and for me, the real freediving showstopper is the journey below the surface to depth.

Before I get all starry-eyed, let me break it down. Depth is also divided into different disciplines: free immersion (FI), constant weight (CWT), constant weight bi-fins (CWTB) and constant weight no fins (CNF).

Free immersion involves the diver pulling themselves down the line, usually a weighted rope descending from a buoy or platform. For constant weight, the monofin comes out, and with this one fin, divers can reach truly incredible depths. This is especially beautiful to watch – the power of the athlete mixed with their grace in the water.

They can also use bi-fins, switching from the dolphin kick of the monofin to the scissor kick of bi-fins.

No fins is special and sometimes considered the purest of disciplines. No equipment, the divers propel themselves down into the depth with that breaststroke-type kick and keyhole stroke as in the pool. It's also the most physically and technically demanding discipline because it requires a high rate of work and a long dive time. While constant weight is beautiful to watch for its power and grace, no fins, done well, is hypnotising, a poem of movement in water. I've had the fortune of seeing some of the top athletes in the discipline descend the line in front of me. Effortless, efficient and exquisite, it is nothing short of, excuse the pun, breathtaking.

Of course, walking into Freedive Utila, I knew none of this. I just thought of those Aussie lads and their lazy kicks as they cruised into that cave. I wanted to know how to do that. I wanted to try that, I needed to learn how ...

So I did.

♦ ♦ ♦

I didn't realise what I was starting with that beginners course. I was neither good nor bad at it. I was competitive but probably more with myself than the others with me on the buoy. I learned that I'm a rare hands-free equaliser – I can equalise my ears by involuntarily opening my eustachian tubes (you're trying that right now, aren't you?). I just give the smallest of yawns with my mouth still closed and that does the trick!

'It might work now but you'll probably have to switch to a different method in the water tomorrow if you want to go a little bit deeper,' my instructor, Tex, advised.

The next day I pretended to pinch my nose but equalised my way: it felt better. I hit the limit of the beginners course, 21 metres. Then I did it again, this time forgetting to pretend to pinch. Tex laughed when he caught me out. 'It's cool but it might not last.'

I'll stick with it until it stops working, I thought. I still am a hands-free equaliser today.

I can't say what it was about those first few weeks

on Utila but they changed me. Yes, I loved it, yes, I was hooked, but I fully expected the passion to fade once I disembarked into a rainy Dublin. Like all the people I'd met, the romances I'd had, the activities I'd done, the early starts and overnight buses, it would be relegated to the *When I was travelling* box of memories. I'd sometimes reminisce, I'd often think of it fondly, but ultimately time and *real life* would lessen the passion, fade out the feelings of achievement, of freedom, and it would simply become 'something cool I did once'.

But it didn't quite work out like that. I couldn't shake it. Once back in Ireland, in the puppet theatre I tried out mermaid puppets, trying to emulate the movements I'd seen and experienced. I found a diving buddy and started practising in the pool – definitely less fun but a good way to run drills, train my breathhold and start melting down my wooden shoulders so I could bend myself into a more streamlined position. It seemed I needed to do things, exercises that kept me involved in the sport on some level. I was desperate not to lose the connection to it or how it made me feel. I started paying more attention to how I breathed, putting time aside in my day to train low and slow deliberate breaths. I practised breathholds in my bed, long tables or sequences of timed breathholds that put me through my paces without having to lift my head from my pillow. I did the (NEVER FUN) apnea walks, which involve finding the balance between efficiency of energy and movement as you walk as far as you can on a breathhold. I trained in the gym. And then I started looking at flights. I wanted to know more. I wanted to experience more.

I made the pilgrimage from Ireland to Utila twice after that. In the summer of 2016 for six weeks, and by the start of 2017, I was ready to go out and spend eight months there. I wanted to become an instructor. I wanted to feel what working away at depth for a period of time felt like. Looking back, I was clueless and my approach was unstructured, but I was hungry.

This sport was different. It forced me to ask more of myself. Not physically, funnily enough, but mentally. It asked me to be honest with myself, to slow down and, instead of trying to quash how I feel and plough on regardless, to bring my body and mind in line with one another. Asking myself how I was and actually listening to the answer, feeling it throughout my body instead of reading it in the ticker tape of headlines that ran across the screen in my mind in line with one another. Merging, marrying the two, was far scarier a prospect than holding my breath underwater. Yes, freediving was something I was intrigued by and wanted to do more of, but most of all, it was a sport, a structure that I needed.

chapter 4

SECOND MOST DANGEROUS SPORT IN THE WORLD

'Lose concentration for a split second and you're gone.

'Today we're going to be talking about freediving, one of the most dangerous sports in the world. For those of you unfamiliar with the sport, it's basically scuba-diving but without the apparatus. You take a big breath and go down on just the air in your lungs, pulling yourself down on a rope or swimming down as far as you can. And remember, once you get down, you have to still get back up. It doesn't sound very relaxing, does it? No, it sounds utterly stressful ... even panic-inducing!

'Yet many freedivers talk about the meditative side of the sport. You must need an incredible amount of self-trust to reach that level of relaxation in such an environment. Surely, an amazing amount of concentration and confidence in your abilities in the water, and indeed the odds, are required. Think about it, you're down at depth, the light from the surface fading, the temperature of the water swallowing you up, dropping. Aside from the jellyfish who float by your narrow window of vision, you're on your own with nothing but the decreasing air in your lungs, completely at the whim of Mother Nature. It's another world entirely.

'It is, by its very nature, such a risky endeavour. I suppose when you're practising it or competing in it, the danger is taken as a given, somewhat normalised so that you can concentrate on tactics and techniques involved. But when you peel it all back to its root, its fundamental element, you're underwater on your own power and that's it. You're a hiccup away from tragedy.

'So what can go wrong? Well, lots of things. Blackouts are very common in freediving. Blackouts are dangerous enough on land but add the "underwater" element and the risk assessment goes off the charts! If you black out underwater it's an almost certainly fatal situation. You're in grave danger of dying. If you don't black out you can have what's called a hypoxic fit. This is a sort of full body convulsion that happens due to low oxygen.

'All sounds pretty extreme, doesn't it? You're right. In fact, it's one of the most extreme sports in the world and ranked as the second most dangerous. Want to know more? Welcome to the world of freediving ...'

Back in Ireland, I couldn't believe what I was hearing. Listening to this introduction was like a dream where the familiar and comforting suddenly morphed into the grotesque and nightmarish. These presenters relishing the sensational and describing their perception of freediving: *stressful, extreme, tragedy, grave danger, black out, convulsion, most dangerous sport in the world,* the words harsh to the ear, making me flinch with each delivery. I struggled to recognise the sport they were describing, let alone feel pulled towards it. *Breathhold,* sure. *Underwater,* check, but this screeching-siren approach not only disguised the allure of the sport, but contorted the danger involved, blowing some elements out of proportion and minimising others.

I wanted to scream, *No, no, no! You've got it all wrong!* at the radio, but I also wanted to hear what else they were going to say. Would freediving be redeemed? Would freedivers be painted as other than death-wish-, thrill-seeking underwater cowboys? Would they mention the calmness, the control, the power, the softness, the freedom?

They didn't. There's nothing sexy about softness.

It's no wonder that so many are curious at best and appalled at worst at the notion of freediving.

There is, of course, a risk involved in freediving. You're holding your breath and you're underwater. Blackouts and LMCs are an element to consider in freediving, especially when breathhold gets pushed too close to its limit. Loss of motor control, or LMC, is the 'hypoxic fit' the presenters were referencing. It occurs after surfacing if oxygen levels are too low. A minor LMC will last just a few seconds and will mainly induce light, uncontrolled head movements, while a severe LMC can affect your whole body and lead to an inability to maintain your airways out of the water.

A blackout happens when you hit a point where there is not enough oxygen left for the body to function normally. Your brain enters into a state of 'survival mode' and you fall unconscious. The brain gradually shuts down all processes in order to prioritise all remaining oxygen for itself. I have, although not proudly, experienced two blackouts during competition on the surface of the water. For anyone in doubt of the power of thought, go underwater with adrenaline fuelling your movements and mentally run through some 'what if' scenarios.

You won't be long chewing through your oxygen supplies.

Blacking out doesn't hurt. It's not an unpleasant sensation at all – like nodding off to sleep on the bus, you're unaware of it happening. The fright, confusion and consequences come when you're being woken up by the driver and you've missed your stop. In freediving, the bus driver is the safety diver and, in my case, they have 'woken me up' with, thankfully, nothing more than my ego being damaged.

Without safety divers or an experienced dive buddy, a blackout or an LMC will have entirely different consequences. You won't spontaneously regain consciousness when submerged in water. If there is no one to bring you to the surface, keep you up out of the water until you start breathing again, freediving lives up to its 'most dangerous sport' reputation.

If I could fill a chapter of this book only repeating one sentence, it would be the number-one rule of freediving.

NEVER DIVE ALONE.

I could fill pages and pages with just these three words, and still it would not hammer home the importance of this rule.

'Yeah, but I was only just –' That's how every justification starts.

There is no 'just'. There is no depth or discipline that is 100 per cent safe to carry out on your own in the water.

There is always a risk, but all risks can be calculated. From their beginner course, each new diver is drilled on the safety elements and rules and, in an ideal world, is equipped with the knowledge and awareness to make good decisions: ones without ego that will not push them beyond their abilities, that will not endanger them or their buddy/safety diver. Each newly certified diver is released into the water world in the hope that they're not going to put themselves in a situation where shortcuts are taken, rules are stretched, 'only just's are muttered and what can be a safe sport becomes high risk. Proper courses by qualified professionals are so important in learning to freedive. In a world where we google how to do most things or watch a YouTube video to learn a new skill, freediving should always be an anomaly.

The people you dive with are probably the most important part of your training: these people will be your buddies, your safety divers. Together you'll head out, set up the buoy from which you'll be diving. You'll inform them of your dive plan – 'I will be doing this dive, to this depth and it'll take me this amount of time.' They might set the line to the correct depth, allowing you time to relax and prepare for your dive. They will accompany you on the last part of your dive, meeting you on your ascent and watching as you surface. A buddy should be someone you trust, who can trust you and who you can communicate with. They are responsible for your safety, and you are responsible for theirs. A buddy will also be the person that high fives you, covers you in splashes on the surface and celebrates later with 'PB cake' when you do a personal best. You can become invested in their dives, their training, and they in yours. Together you debrief, maybe problem-solve. But most of all, connections and friendships are made with the people you dive with, the people you head out to the blue, set up and share a buoy with. My freediving buddies are scattered all over the world, but I will hop from one foot to the other with excitement when the time comes for us to be reunited in the big blue.

There are lots of different ways to dive – line training, on the reef or in and out through caves. Each activity becomes far safer when you've an awareness of your abilities, the variables, the conditions and confidence to say 'no, not today'.

Most people that have been diving for any length of time will have been involved in a rescue, whether it is as a safety diver in a competition, as an instructor or coach or even as a training buddy. As divers and athletes push themselves further and further, it becomes a greater possibility.

Maybe your buddy pushed themselves too much, took too long on a dive – there are so many combinations of variables that can lead a diver to have an LMC or a blackout. The main thing is that, in most cases, both divers are conscious and chatting about it soon afterwards.

There have been fatalities in freediving. Some incredible athletes, world-class divers, have lost their lives freediving. There are books, documentaries and tributes that describe their circumstances far better than I will attempt to.

I don't claim to know any of them personally. I did have contact with fellow Irish person Stephen Keenan. Steve was a well-respected diver who organised the safety for some of the most prestigious freediving competitions in the world. He'd moved from

Dublin and set up his own freediving school in Dahab. Anyone who has spent time in Dahab will have a Steve story, many of them a combination of diving, divilment, Dubs ... and drinks!

The first seed of visiting Dahab was sown in early summer of 2017. I was in Utila and sharing my freediving personal bests on Facebook. With each new depth reached, Steve would message me, congratulate me and ask me about the dive. There seemed to be a genuine interest, a wish to promote the sport, particularly among people from our little Emerald Isle.

He was heading off to Vertical Blue in Dean's Blue Hole, the Bahamas, to be chief of safety. I was curious to meet this Dub who had progressed so much in the sport, represented our country and was now one of the most respected safety divers in the world. His reputation extended far beyond Dublin or Dahab.

On 16 July 2017, I messaged Steve. Dublin were playing Kildare in the Leinster Senior Football final. Not that I was a big GAA fan, but when you're away, these things take on a different meaning. There was slagging – especially when Dublin clinched the title by six points. I was sorry I'd messaged ...

The following Saturday, I came in off the boat from the morning's session. A student was waiting for me to pull me aside. She'd been in Dahab the previous year and trained with Steve in Dahab Freedivers. She told me about the accident in the Blue Hole.

I didn't know Steve bar a few message exchanges,

but the ripples of his death were felt throughout the freediving community. Over the next few years I would meet people that had considered him a dear friend, I'd visit his dive centre, I'd dive in the Blue Hole, and I'd hear many stories about the blue-eyed Dub.

Each fatality is not due to just one thing, but a series of incidents that lead to the accident. These accomplished, widely respected and much-loved divers paid the ultimate price of their lives. It seems disrespectful to them, their legacy and our sport to think that we might be the exception, that we can operate outside the rules and procedures created to keep us safe in this sport that we love. That we are somehow exempt and can venture out alone, whether it is in 10 metres or 100, and think ...

'I was only just –'

chapter 5

YATBA' – TO FOLLOW

'You're going where?'

'Dahab.'

'Where's that?'

'Egypt.'

'Ah, Claire!'

I was in my friends Charlotte and Louise's house, filling them in on my latest travel plans. They were used to me heading off. I'd spent months away in South and Central America in 2015. The following year I had returned to Utila for six weeks to freedive more. Then at the start of 2017, I packed up fully, sold as many belongings as possible and headed out to live on Utila for eight months.

These travels, my adventures as I called them, particularly this one, were usually knee-jerk reactions, often done on the spur of the moment, a response to feeling like I didn't fit in at home for a multitude of reasons. I had returned from Honduras to celebrate Mum's 60th birthday. Eight months was the longest time I'd spent away, and I had missed my family so much. Lying in my little room in the guest house on Utila, with a fan pointed directly at me, a feeble attempt to keep me cool, I regularly had dreams that I woke up in my old bedroom in Leixlip. I could hear my family downstairs; I could hear the sounds out on the road beyond my curtain. I'd go to swing my legs out of the bed to head down for a cup of tea ... and then I'd wake up. Waking always took a moment of readjustment when I remembered where I was. I was so happy to be there, in that guest house with a dock that backed right onto the water. Each day was spent swimming, floating, playing, diving – all in the water. I was seldom out of my bikini. I didn't yearn to be back in Ireland, but I missed my family. And Mum celebrates her birthday in style, never confined to one day, and birthdays with a zero in them are different events, dinners, occasions spread out over the weeks after. It was something I didn't want to miss.

But arriving home from that trip at the end of September 2017, I didn't feel *at home*. It's like looking at your home town, the place you grew up in, spent years of your life in, through the eyes of a stranger. It was unrecognisable, yet also 'nothing's changed' achingly familiar.

I couldn't see or find the groove to settle myself into. Beyond catching up with everyone, I didn't know how to slot myself back into life there, how to busy myself. My family was changing; Katie had told me she was pregnant. A baby! It was hard to imagine. So ... grown up, and a real indicator that she was part of a new family now: one she was creating herself. Sarah was carving her career out successfully in London and living with Paul. Matt was busy with college and heading into the final year of his architecture degree ... And there was I, single and holding my breath.

It felt so trivial, that I was becoming a self-parody. Perhaps that's exactly what it was, something I had latched onto to fill the void. My work in the theatre, the rollercoaster ride that is pantomime season, didn't start until mid-November. I was home with nothing to do. Plunged straight back into the what-am-I-doing feeling, I didn't have the answers. Once again, I felt in limbo.

So I found myself seeing Charlotte's and Louise's faces in person instead of on a blurry poor-connection FaceTime screen and, at the same time, telling them about my plans to travel to Egypt the following week.

'I'm only going for five weeks this time,' I countered.

This was *definitely* in the kick-the-can-down-the-road category but, with a little bit of denial, I could disguise it as 'Oh, would ya look, an opportunity for more freediving!' More freediving, a balm for my soul and time for me to recalibrate, get a sense of who I was before I came home and compared myself to my family.

'But Egypt? Is that not really dangerous?'

This was not my first time hearing this since I'd booked my flights two days previously. It sort of baffled me. In the last two and half years I'd been through Panama, Colombia, Ecuador, Peru, Mexico, Guatemala, Belize and Honduras. What was it about Egypt that scared people far more than these countries? I wasn't trying to be deliberately obtuse or naive. Many of the previous spots had their own reputations and 'danger statistics'. San Pedro Sula, Honduras, has been in and out of the top ten of cities for homicide rate.

But in Egypt, there was the threat of terrorism.

I'd met freedivers that summer who'd travelled to Egypt, Dahab specifically, for diving. Some came from the UK, some from Europe, and some had gone so far as to base themselves out there. My flights were booked so I wasn't going to change my mind. I felt that Freedive Utila had taught me all it could about freediving and that Dahab would kick off the next phase, whatever that might be.

I was going.

The flight to Sharm el Sheikh through Istanbul felt a mere hop, skip and jump in comparison to the three-day boat–bus–flight–overnight-layover–flight trek that it takes to get from Utila to Dublin. Coming through security, I was in a queue of people all carrying oddly shaped bags. *Monofins!* I'd never seen that before. Excitement fighting and winning over tiredness,

I was sure these other freedivers were also heading to Dahab. It began to sink in: Dahab really might be the Mecca of freediving. I left the airport in the middle of the night pushing my own assortment of oddly shaped, I-can't-pack-lightly-to-save-my-life bags. The doors opened revealing a gauntlet of men standing with signs, hustling for our attention shouting, '*Taxi! Taxi!*'

Beyond them, the darkness of the sky was different. The smell was different; the warmth was different. The drivers' attire of white galabeyas was different. Immediately sweating in my 'Irish October' travel outfit, I looked for the taxi driver my friend had organised from Dahab. I followed him reluctantly to his car, relying heavily on the fact that this girl I sort of knew trusted him, pushing questionable safety thoughts out of my head – there was no time for that now. I had no choice.

Waking up the next morning, my flatmate had left a note: she was going to the Blue Hole and would be back around noon. I didn't know what the story was – was it safe to go out on your own? I hoped so because I was starving. I ventured across the road, looking for Wi-Fi and trying to figure out the exchange rate for Egyptian pounds. My eyes scanned the Arabic letters over shop doorways but I had to poke my nose inside to see if they were somewhere that might sell food. I didn't have to go far before I stumbled across a restaurant attached to a dive shop. I pointed at the picture for chips – it was the only thing I recognised.

Not my breakfast of choice, but I'd been awake most of the last 24 hours, so they'd do! I'd settle, sleep and then become more adventurous with my food choices. No matter how much I'd travelled the past while, the first day I always felt tentative and disorientated. But Dahab, more than anywhere I'd been, within days felt like home.

♦ ♦ ♦

12 October, journal entry

Claire,

You're here now. Good idea, bad idea, you're here. Give it all you have. Open yourself up. Allow yourself to find and feel happiness.

You're stuck ... you know that; your tummy, your throat, your shoulders. Held and stuck.

Stuck with the unsaid. Emotions that are churning and feel so big. How can they possibly all fit inside?

Let's play a little game ... *What if?*

What if everything you needed right now was here, in Dahab. In the magnificent Blue Hole, in the fiery sunset sky, in the warm waters, in the routine, in the activities, in the people.

What if you had all the ingredients in front of you, at your disposal, you were lacking in nothing ... what would you do?

You're curious about competing. Something sparked in Utila in all your time there. *What if* you explore that? *What if* you explore giving yourself permission to try, to experience and not concern yourself with what others might think? *What if* it didn't matter what depth you do?

What if you did it just for you?

What if this is just the beginning?

♦ ♦ ♦

I hadn't come to Dahab with the intention of competing. I barely knew what was involved. I had seen a competition, a world championship in fact, and had been in awe of the set-up. A competition was taking place in a few weeks in the Blue Hole. It would be more informal than a world championship and, maybe, the perfect place to start.

Like my approach to most things, particularly ones that scare me, I started breaking it down into steps. What would I need to do? I had all the equipment and I could determine the depth I wanted to do based on how I was feeling right up to the night before, when I would announce my dive.

My training sessions took on a new structure. I practised doing one or two warm-ups and then going for one dive. I had my buddy give me a countdown to my official start time.

'Three minutes to Official Top.'

I carried out my familiar preparation inside this different framework.

'One minute to Official Top.'

'Twenty seconds.'

'Ten, nine, eight …'

There was something about hearing a countdown that made my heart beat faster. I was going to have to really focus on my relaxation next time.

'*Official Top!*'

On 24 October 2017, the morning of my first competition dive, I slept late. I was used to diving first thing in the morning and on an empty stomach. With my dive in the afternoon, I'd have to change that up. I lay in bed, switching between reading and doing short meditations on my Buddhify app. I had my routine marked out. I'd get up at 11, stretch and put my gear, already laid out, into my bag. This felt like no nerves I'd experienced before. I'd always get nervous before a show or if the choir had a big performance, but I used the energy: I knew how to channel the adrenaline rush into the performance. This was different. I didn't want any surges in adrenaline. Putting my earphones in, I put on a mellow playlist and moved slowly through my stretches. Singing along helped. It stopped me holding my breath before it was time.

I hopped in a taxi, throwing my bag and fins into the back.

'Blue Hole, please.' We started winding through the streets out towards the road that led to the Blue Hole.

Just before we were about to turn, a local scuba instructor and Dahab resident nicknamed Barracuda skidded in front of the car on his bike. I knew him to say hi to, to stop and chat with. He called me Irish, something I imagine he had called his friend Steve Keenan.

'Stop, stop, stop!'

'What the f–?'

He spoke quickly to the driver in Arabic and shouted in at me, 'Follow.'

Jesus, what is he at? Is he messing? What's going on? I had one eye on my watch and the other on where Barracuda was leading us. I desperately hoped we'd be on our way soon. You have to check in one hour before your Official Top. I'd left plenty of time to spare, but this detour was eating into that time and, more pressingly, doing nothing for my nerves.

We came to an abrupt stop outside a house and Barracuda disappeared inside. *Do we wait? Does he want to come with us?*

Barracuda came tripping out and thrust a bag in at me through the open window. 'Good luck in your dive.'

'What –?'

'I want it back but have it for today. It's the Irish flag – it was Steve's.'

The car had already taken off before I had words to say other than a stunned 'Thank you'. Tears spilled down my cheeks at the gesture all the way to the Blue Hole as I held the flag, this precious flag, on my lap.

Dressed in my wetsuit, I adjusted my weight belt

before heading into the water. A few divers stopped by my bay in Aqua Marina to wish me luck.

'Steve's flag?' one asked.

I nodded.

They kissed their hand and gently touched the flag folded beside me. 'Here, let me help you with that.' They distributed my weights evenly around my back and walked me down to the water. 'Good luck.'

Diving in a competition felt very different to any of the diving I'd done previously. It was the same spot, the Blue Hole, that I'd been training in for a few weeks but suddenly it was all ... official.

Equipment checks, sign-in times, warm-up slots and then the all-important Official Top. Having to dive at a specific time, not just when I felt ready, was so new.

I felt the nerves and energy of the set-up but I focused on my relaxation. Lying on the surface, face down with my snorkel in my mouth, I sang, 'Cos you're a sky, cos you're a sky full of stars.'

I let the sounds of the people around me, the judges, the other divers, the safety divers, float away and focused on the song I was singing in my head.

'Such a heavenly viiiiiew ...'

I opened my eyes and looked down: it really was. I'd only been here three and a half weeks but I understood why freedivers from all over the world flocked here. Closing my eyes again, I focused on the images of this now familiar place and blocked out the unfamiliar set-up.

The dive felt easy: it *was* easy. It felt relaxed and that more was well within reach.

I'm okay.

I pulled the tag from inside my hood and showed the judges ... and then I waited. Part of the surface protocol is that the judges wait for 30 seconds from surfacing to make a decision, basically to make sure you can keep yourself up out of the water. I glanced around at the safety divers who were nearby, smiling.

White card!

The judges had deemed it a clean dive with no penalties. I had earned my first white card. My first competition dive, my first white card ... and my first national record. I would go on to break another national record but this one, my first, was special.

I was covered in splashes of celebration.

All thoughts of what anyone might think went out the window. This was an achievement, and though not everyone might understand it, I was proud.

In fact, I was elated. This signified little wins that were so much bigger than the Velcro tag in my hand.

This was a different side of freediving, a different way of challenging myself. It wasn't something I could achieve by bulldozing my way through, by physically preparing but neglecting, pushing down the mental preparations. You had to do both simultaneously.

Wrapping myself in the tricolour, Steve's tricolour, I smiled and took pictures. This was a moment I'd want to remember. I had two more dives left to do, two more opportunities for national records, but I knew that beyond them something new had been ignited.

I wanted to try more.

chapter 6

THE THING WITH FEATHERS

I burrowed further into the cocoon of duvets I'd assembled on my bed, pushing empty crisp wrappers and the remnants of selection boxes over the edge onto the ground below.

Christmas 2017 I had moved in with my aunty Helen into my granny's old house. It was great not to be under Mum and Dad's feet and it certainly was closer to the theatre. The house would be going up for sale shortly so it was a temporary solution. I was grateful for the pitstop but it did nothing to help with my sense of displacement.

You're not going to feel secure if you keep kicking the can down the road and fecking off travelling.

Fuck off! I didn't want to hear it, even if it was from me.

I had come back from Dahab, from the sun and the success of my first freediving competition, and straight onto the conveyor belt of performances in the pantomime season. I loved the Christmas show, I really did. Lambert Puppet Theatre was decked out in Christmas decorations and, no matter what's going on, I can't help but soften at the sight of a Christmas tree and fairy lights. Kids were wild with excitement and sugar but became transfixed by the puppets the theatre was famous for. It plucked the nostalgia strings of my own childhood, of going to the pantomime with my cousins and even to the theatre itself. There was something magical about it. The first and second times we performed that show in front of an audience was always a thrill. By the 30th and 40th time, the shine had worn off.

My back and shoulders ached from outstretched arms moving puppets over my head. My voice was croaky and scratched my throat, on the verge of disappearing before the final performances.

But the puppet theatre was a good way to spend Christmas, in a way. It masked the fact that I'd not much else to do.

New Year's Day, a day off, I scrolled through photos idly on my phone, distracting myself from the distraction of Netflix. I came across a photo of my trip to Dahab three months previously. Me, fresh out of the water, face split by a wide smile. Who was that girl? I barely recognised her, her unbridled joy and chin tilted to the sky. I almost resented her. How can someone go from that to – I looked around at the desolate little nest I'd built around me: the cup of wine on the bedside locker, the piles of clothes on the floor – *this* in such a short space of time.

I wasn't stupid – I saw the pattern: travelling, the adventures that all were planned and booked when I felt too worn down to find a way through in 'normal' life. I'd go away, build myself up, come back with renewed confidence, a stronger sense of self ... only for it to ebb away within weeks of landing home.

I wanted to live in Ireland, I really did – my family and friends were there. But in Ireland I couldn't seem to find any momentum. I'd fall into a pattern of getting by, each win, each step of progress, small and insignificant compared to the all-encompassing feelings of depression and futility that frequently engulfed me.

Funny, I don't say or write that word very often. Depression. I'm not afraid of it but I still think it's not big enough to describe what happens when I say I feel that way. I'm not just feeling a bit sad – I'm feeling SadAngryGuiltyAshamed EmbarassedEmptyHopeless ListlessTiredParanoidApatheticSensitive ...

I suppose it's one of those if-you-know-you-know situations.

I wanted my family to know. It's a catch-22: I needed them to know, to understand, but at the same time I wouldn't ever want them to. To know it is to experience it and I couldn't, can't, bear the thought of any one of my five people feeling like I have. I wanted to protect them from it – and, more importantly, from me when I'm like this.

I first noticed something was wrong, something was different, the summer after I finished college. I took on double shifts in a job as a carer to save money for a master's degree and a move to London. At the start it was easy to blame tiredness. I was working throughout the day and often during the night, snatching hours of sleep whenever I could. Maybe it was a result of moving around in people's homes, trying to be as unintrusive as possible, but I felt sort of invisible, like the colour had faded out of me. I felt less sure about things, and the blustering confidence of finishing a drama degree actually knowing what my next step was quickly dissipated. I'd spend nights with my boyfriend of the time, squashed into his single bed, lying on my side crying. I had no explanation – there was no sobbing or even sounds. It was like taking off your coat and bag when you came in from work: this was just something I needed to do at the end of the day.

I didn't have a name for it. There was always an event or circumstance I could use to explain away the feelings or, sure, if in doubt, blame it on tiredness.

The next few years – going to London for my master's, coming home the minute it was done, moving in with my boyfriend, breaking up with my boyfriend – saw the symptoms expand and rotate. In one way I appeared so confident, so comfortable in people's company, outgoing, and in other ways, I got so nervous at the prospect of going out. I replayed conversations again and again and again and berated myself for not standing up for myself, for not being funnier, kinder, prettier, more charming, quieter – anything other than the way I had been. I dealt with difficult feelings by eating ... or not. My weight and appearance started to mirror the patterns. Funnily, often that's what people would notice, express concern for: putting on or losing weight. There's a strange comfort in the tangible. Often I'd think to myself, *The weight is the least of my problems – you'd want to see what's going on inside my head.*

I knew the weight wasn't the root cause. I just didn't know what was.

Finally I went to see my GP. I had fainted at work and went to get checked out. Look, I had been to an all-girl's school. We went to talks and received information about eating disorders. With hindsight and more knowledge about the nuances of disordered eating and body-image issues, it's obvious to me that food became a coping mechanism. But at the time, I was still a healthy weight and doing nothing extreme in terms of controlling or bingeing food. But I had raised a red flag with my doctor. She referred me to a doctor in St Patrick's hospital that specialised in eating disorders. I first met Dr Griffin when I was 24. He quickly ruled out any eating disorders but wasn't so quick to dismiss the other symptoms.

The second half of my twenties were the bad, blurry years. I cycled through denial, wild, impetuous decisions, highly charged anxiety and long bouts of crippling depression. Awake at night and sleeping through the day, I shut my curtains, made excuse after excuse why I couldn't meet up or go to dinner. The mask of *everything's fine, I have it under control* was so important to me but, fuck, it was slipping.

I was candid about my diagnosis, depression. I spoke, albeit detachedly, about my treatment, regular check-ins with Dr Griffin and daily medication, but the real focus was on limiting what people saw. 'Depression', in theory, is neat and tidy, a clear box to fit into. It's manifestation, on the other hand, how it looked on a day-to-day basis, was a gnarled and pitiful beast that I was not willing to expose anyone to. I was committed and complicit in keeping it as my dirty secret ... until I couldn't anymore.

I don't always know how to ask for help, and I can see people don't always know how to give it. There's a long history of misunderstanding, or maybe lack of understanding. Are they the same thing? They feel different.

I'd see it in my family's eyes, their reactions reflecting how I'd changed, and even through the fog I could tell they were walking on eggshells around me. I so desperately wanted to be understood. I wanted them to know my daily fight because it sometimes felt like a battle I was losing. I was angry that they couldn't find the words to reach me. I was angry because I could see that maybe those words didn't exist.

I always said, 'I don't need to talk about it all the time. I just need to know that there's space for me to if I need it.' I knew for my friends and my family it was veering into dangerous and uncomfortable territory, not because they didn't care but because they didn't always know what to say and they ran the risk of stepping on a saying-the-wrong-thing landmine.

I wanted to scream.

I knew when I was being negative. I knew that it wasn't *all* bad. I knew that but the message kept getting diverted before it hit my brain and then I would feel so guilty for knowing it but not feeling it. Do you think I didn't know? I did. I didn't want to be like this, feel like this, have my limbs feel leaden and heavy, my eyes move at a never-quite-quick-enough pace. I felt utterly useless. The pressure to compensate was my only motivation but it would eventually catch up on me and I would crash.

Each crash looked different. Sometimes it was a stop. A ringing in my ears, a numbness, a detachment. Sometimes it was an onslaught of emotions that were so unbearable I wanted to run my nails across my face, my arms, just to feel it somewhere other than inside. Sometimes it was sleep, hours spent on the cusp of consciousness, never fully awake, never fully alert.

'Are you not doing what your counsellor told you to do?'

I understood the question, but in that moment I often felt like a child that's not done their homework and has to suffer the inevitable consequences.

I didn't have a timeline for this – depression, mental illness, bipolar disorder, borderline personality disorder, whatever it was. I didn't know when I would be able to tick the box marked 'better'. But I did know it could be part of my life for a long time to come. I just may (hopefully) learn to live with it better.

But I was tired, and most of all, I was scared.

That's what I wanted them to know, my family, my friends: I was scared. This was a frightening state to be in, and at times, it was hard to manage on my own. I longed for someone who would share my bed and when those nights came, would just remind me that it would pass. He would anchor me in reality, not making it all better with a stroke of a magical mental-illness wand, but he would be there. He'd remind me of the good qualities I have when all I could see were the bad. Doing this on my own was terrifying.

I think it's hard to love and care for someone with a mental illness. Campaigns would have us believe it's as simple as 'just talk to someone' and the healing begins. I'd been in this cycle for 13 years now, and I knew it wasn't always the case. The person doesn't always know what to say, doesn't always say the right thing. They shouldn't be condemned for that, but the nature of the beast is that the illness doesn't always let you process information in the most rational way. A seemingly innocuous, well-intentioned statement can hit hard, set off a spiral of guilt and shame and make you want to retreat further and further.

I did talk to my parents, my sisters, my brother and sometimes my friends, but mainly I talked to my counsellor, Sarah, a wonderful woman I've seen for years. Someone who holds space for me, helps me detangle my messy thoughts and feelings but always reminds me that I have the tools to do so myself. It's strange having a relationship with someone who knows everything about me that I'd dare to say out loud, but who I've never seen outside of her house.

I'm so keenly aware that my pain is also my family's pain. I know this, that this illness has caused conflict, arguments and probably more worry than I have a clue about. They say that suffering is made up of two parts: pain and lack of acceptance. By not accepting you're compounding the pain and it becomes suffering. I was working on accepting myself, where I was at. It would take a while for me to get there with my family, accepting and not blaming myself for what they went through with me, go through with me, what I bring to the table just by being me. I know it's not the most compassionate of self-talk, but at times I felt like such a burden.

Cue 'but it's not my fault' rage … aaand we're right back at the start of the rollercoaster ride. Please make sure your seatbelt is securely fastened and keep your arms and legs inside the carriage at all times.

I wrote out the poem 'The Guest House' by Rumi in my journal in the first few days of 2018. It describes something my dad has always said, but in his way.

'How are you feeling?'

'Bad.'

'Bad, bad?'

'Yeah … unfortunately.'

'Okay, what do we need to do?'

'I don't know, I'll be grand. It is what it is. No different to last time … and the time before. It'll pass.'

'Well, let the feelings in, give them a cup of tea, sit them down and see what they want. Then usher them gently and politely on their way.'

'I can do that.'

'I'll check in later on.'

I liked it. It normalised this giant wave of emotion but puts you in the driving seat. You don't have to have the legs knocked from underneath you. You can just bunch yourself up, maybe not play in the waves, but dive under or float in the surf … and when you're ready, turn to the shore and move steadily towards it. Know when to get out of the water.

In the single bed in my granny's box room, surrounded by empty crisp wrappers and red-wine-stained teacups, I felt lost, I felt lonely. I was angry, raging and hopeless. The wave was coursing through me as a violent 'spring-cleaning'. Maybe clearing the way for better things, a new path.

Hope is such a funny little thing. I've always

struggled with the term, understanding the word but without fully being able to understand the concept, to recognise it in my body, in my being.

Just have hope.

I'd shake my head and nod at the same time in hurried I-want-to-bring-this-conversation-to-a-close agreement.

Oh yeah, no. Totally.

Right now, with barely enough energy to get out of bed and go to the bathroom, hope was an abstract concept that was worlds away from the stale-smelling sheets I had burrowed into.

Asking a person who might not see the point of getting out of bed that morning, or having a shower or brushing their teeth, eating – the basics, fundamentals of self-care. Asking them to have hope, telling them that there is hope, well, you may as well ask them to read something in a language they don't speak, to solve a complex maths equation. It is just beyond their capabilities at that moment.

So for me, I had to make things tangible. I had to make *hope* things, people.

Hope is my first nephews, as I call them – my friends Charlotte and Louise's two beautiful boys.

I *hope* to dance embarrassingly at their 21sts. I want to tell them that when they were a few weeks old, I was the first person, aside from their mothers, to do a tandem dream feed. They will know that story *back to front* and will roll their eyes each time I tell it.

Hope is my sister Katie's baby, due in four months' time.

That growing bump holds someone I feel I already know simply because I know their mum. I know every micro movement of Katie's face and what it might mean. I've shared a bed with her as a child. I've kicked and wrestled and, at one time, in a strange burst of strength, flung her against a wall. She has been my companion, my competitor and by my side for all of her life. I want to see this little person grow up, this child that is half Katie, half her husband, someone whose gentle manner and chatty nature I respect and have grown to hold just as dear.

I looked back at that smiling picture of me in Dahab having just achieved two national records in a sport that has helped me to begin to understand concepts of strength and resilience I thought I was automatically disqualified from. That is hope. With a trickle of warmth from within, I began to feel it: that sense of pride, that absolute full-bodied feeling of achievement, of accomplishment, of putting myself out there and doing it. Not a screed of make-up and, quite frankly, my brows could do with comb ... Still. I'm not looking at my body shape or size in the wetsuit. I'm looking at a smile that radiates a host of positive emotions. That smile as wide as my face will allow.

This photo took on a significance, a sort of a visual reminder that 'this too shall pass'.

For the days (and maybe even weeks) when I

struggled to put on a bra and runners to go for the walk that I'd been assured would do me 'the power of good', I could look at this photo, remind myself that how I feel isn't who I am, that I am capable of so much more and that this smile will return and that the girl who does cool things will someday soon resurface. Or in other words ...

There is hope.

Just keep her goin', Patsy.

chapter 7

FALLING HARD AND FALLING SHORT

January always feels longer than 31 days. A lot longer.

I didn't exactly spring into action with the enthusiasm for a new year, but I did get out of bed. That's a start, eh?

Just as often as I experienced these cycles, I knew when it was time to put one foot in front of the other and start building back up. It took a while – I looked at it as doing little tasks that wouldn't necessarily make tomorrow better, but by next week there'd be a difference. It might've been getting out of bed and putting on clean pyjamas; it might've been cooking a meal, even beans on toast, rather than ordering in pizza. It wasn't always easy but it was familiar.

Sometimes I just flung myself back into my

day-to-day, energy suddenly turned up from zero to ten, working, maybe even socialising. This sounded great, productive and with the semblance of normality, of being *better*, but there was always an edge to it. I'd be jittery and never fully present in the moment, moving through the motions like a *slightly* manic wound-up toy.

Pulling on tracksuit bottoms and a hoodie to shuffle down to the pier in Dún Laoghaire on the morning of the second of January, I knew one thing.

I wanted this year to be different.

I would try to ride it out. I would try to find a way through, start creating a life in Ireland that made me feel happy, like I belonged, the beginnings of roots.

I'll give myself a week or so, I thought, *get the last of the shows out of the way, bank the money and go from there.*

Then on 18 January, 2018, catching myself by surprise, I met a guy.

Trust me, I was as surprised as you are. I met him, quite typically, on a date I had sworn would be my last one. Easy to say after the fact. In the second week of January, I'd gone on a date with this other poor lad. We'd met up but he just needed someone to talk to. He was going through a rough time and couldn't tell his family. His work frowned upon 'that sort of thing' and, out of desperation, he had downloaded Tinder in the hope of finding someone to talk to. I felt like the universe was watching, stifling a giggle.

Very. Fucking. Funny.

It was not what I had had in mind for the evening but I resigned myself to being his ear for the duration of the date. We walked the pier in Dún Laoghaire and stopped to get a cup of tea to warm our hands. My heart went out to the guy, but I was also clear(ish) about my own boundaries and limitations.

'Obviously, this can't go any further, and unfortunately I'm not in a position to offer to be at the end of the phone should you need to chat again. But I can send you some resources, names of organisations you can call if you're open to it? It might be no harm chatting to a professional.'

We hugged goodbye and I declined the offer of a lift, preferring to stroll back home in the beginning of a rare snowfall.

No more – enough, I thought to myself.

I'd a date arranged for later in the week. I'd been chatting to this guy for a few days and we'd moved into the comfier chat-sitting-room of WhatsApp. I deleted Tinder; I wouldn't cancel the date because we'd made an arrangement. But I went into it expecting nothing and having already mentally tapped out of online dating.

Isn't it always the way?

Darragh was from Roscommon so we decided to split the distance and met in a bar halfway between our respective homes. I'd had a busy day, spending most of the time rushing around and always 10 minutes behind. I ended up making a quick pit stop along the way in Leixlip to change out of my reliable leggings and hoodie combo and drag a make-up brush across my face. Grand, presentable. It would do.

Darragh had arrived before me. I spotted him as soon as I got in the door.

Jaaaysus, his pictures did not do him justice. In a weird, almost reverse catfish, he was gorgeous!

It kind of caught me off guard. Dark hair, pale skin and light-blue eyes that sort of twinkled with amusement. I'm fully aware that I'm describing someone that isn't a million miles away from my own colouring. Don't say anything! I know the story of Narcissus and I'm ignoring any of the connotations or red flags that might spring to mind.

I was instantly attracted to this guy.

More than a little bit flustered, I started talking, barely leaving space for a breath, gesticulating wildly as I answered his questions. It wasn't until I hit myself in the face with my own hand that I managed to slow down and take a breath.

But he was smiling at me.

'Sorry, I guess I'm a bit nervous.'

'That's okay, I'm enjoying the show.'

It was one of those rare occasions where the conversation translated from text into real life. We fired quips back and forth, both well able to give as good as we got.

'Touché,' he conceded, lifting his glass in my direction. 'One for the road?'

'Please, tonic water.' I was glad of the breather, my cheeks were flushed and, again, I found myself flustered. *Pull yourself together, Claire.*

We said our goodbyes. The wind had picked up and it had started to lash rain. A quick hug ended the night as we made a dash to our cars.

He ended up driving behind me on the road leading out to the motorway. My phone started ringing and his name flashed on the screen.

'Everything okay?'

'Yeah, pull over at that little shop ahead.'

'What? Is everything okay?'

'Yeah, it's grand. Just pull over.'

Shite, my tail light was probably out or something. There was feck all I could do about it now so what was his deal?

He pulled in behind me and ran up to my car, opening my door.

'Are you okay?' I asked. I hadn't a fecking notion what was going on.

'Yeah, I just wanted to do this …'

He pulled me out of the car and kissed me. On the side of a road, in the lashings of rain, he kissed me.

'… but I'd bottled it before. I'd be kicking myself later if I didn't.'

…

…

…

'Aaaah, okay! Thank you?!'

We both burst out laughing and he sat me back into the car and closed the door.

'G'luck,' and off he went.

I drove home in a daze. *What the fuck just happened?*

Darragh and I continued dating. He was a year or so out of a long-term relationship, a marriage in fact. He had two small children who stayed with him every second weekend. He played rugby those alternate weekends, so we soon settled into a pattern where I'd go up to him during the week for an evening.

I was cautious – well, cautious, for me. I listened to the language he used and was fully aware of his situation and what he may or may not be ready for. I promised myself I'd go along with it, taking each week as it came, and when I felt like I wanted a bit more, I'd check in with him or check out and protect myself.

The conversation came in March. The whole country was covered in unprecedented amounts of snow and the news was full of stories of people snowed in or snowed out the length and breadth of the country. Queues in local supermarkets snaked up and down the aisles as everyone dashed to stock up on bread and wine, the extreme weather bringing out the Last Supper in people. I had headed to Roscommon just before the weather had turned from light sprinkling to *shut the schools, work from home, do not make unnecessary journeys!* We spent the next few days snowed in. It was the longest amount of time we'd spent with each other. He worked during the day, I read and worked on my laptop, and in the evening we wrapped up and went on snow-crunching-underneath-our-feet walks. Later we'd cook together companionably and open a bottle of wine before settling in in front of the fire. It was as nice as it sounds.

I had to pinch myself. This sexy and funny man wanted to spend time with me? It was easy, it was warm, and with that penny-dropping moment, I realised I wanted more. I wanted a boyfriend.

No one likes having the talk, but I needed to know if he saw the potential for it to go somewhere. And that's all it was. Just checking in that he was open to it going somewhere. I knew he enjoyed my company, my humour, but I'd probably need to step away at this point if that's all it was.

He wasn't surprised when I brought it up. We'd seen each other weekly for almost two months. He teased my tentativeness at broaching the subject. We both chose our words carefully, not wanting to be the first to lay our cards on the table, but agreed we'd take it slow. I wasn't brave enough to use a word like 'boyfriend' but that didn't really matter. I was happy enough to be on the same page that we weren't dating anyone else and we'd see where this went.

A few days later, his children were due to visit.

'Ah sure, stay another night – you can't drive home in this and they won't be able to get down.'

They lived a few hours away, and with the weather the way it was, it looked like their visit would be postponed.

The next morning his phone rang. It was his brother offering to go pick up the kids in his 4x4. Darragh jumped at the chance, understandably. He quickly moved onto the next call and began making the necessary arrangements. I couldn't help but overhear him – he was sitting right beside me. I began to panic. If his kids were coming down, I'd have to leave. How the fuck was I going to drive home? I didn't have a 4x4 ...

He spent the next half hour on the phone. I began to surreptitiously make frantic enquiries to local B&Bs while calling home and asking what the roads were like over into Kildare. People sent me back pictures of cars abandoned along the side of the N4.

He was so excited that his children were coming down. I got it, I really did. But he had completely forgotten about me ... and I was mortified. I wanted to get out of there as soon as possible.

'Ah, you don't have to go now – the lads won't be here for a few hours. I'm not kicking you out.'

He wasn't kicking me out, he'd just forgotten me. I felt so ... embarrassed. I wanted to make myself as small as possible and remove myself from the situation as quickly as I could. Once I got into my car I'd figure out what to do.

I said a hurried goodbye and threw my bag onto the passenger seat. I drove out of the estate, pulled in, pulled out my phone and tried to come up with a plan.

I plotted out hotels and guest houses along the way. I would take it slowly and go as far as Potential

Stop Number 1 and then assess the situation. I was reluctant to stay overnight, but if things got too hairy on the road, I would abort the drive. I felt so ... dirty, for the lack of another word. I quashed the feelings, rationalising that his kids came first, that's the way it should be. It was great that he was so excited to see them. But needling in my brain was the speed at which he had compartmentalised, almost looking surprised to still see me there when he got off the phone. I felt like an afterthought and the warm, cosy feelings of the last few days were left behind in Roscommon.

I made it as far as the junction for Leixlip. Brilliant! I'd indicate and go in and stay with Mum and Dad for the night. As soon as I entered the slipway, the road disappeared. Cars were haphazardly parked in different directions along the hard shoulder.

Nope! I'd never make it down to Ryevale if this was how things were. I drove back down the slip road on the other side and continued on the motorway. The M50 was unrecognisable. Reduced to 10 kilometres an hour, I crawled along the road and felt it slip and skid underneath my tyres. Driving was far more hazardous than it had been the whole way down. Making slow, slow progress, I finally exited towards Dún Laoghaire. Stopping in at the Spar to buy provisions (bread and wine) I was so relieved to get home. Helen would be staying at work for the next few days, and I'd be on my own. Still, I could walk to the shops and I had heating. I probably had too much time to think but that's what Netflix was for.

Darragh and I continued our pattern of weekly visits, him occasionally coming to Dublin, where I'd plan trips, hikes and restaurants. I'd plan surprises, thinking outside the box, nights away which he always delighted in. It was all lovely until it was time to go home. An hour or so before, I'd feel his attention shifting: knowing that he was switching modes, he'd start to disengage. I knew we'd send the odd text and maybe have a call in the next few days, but he wouldn't be fully present until I arrived on whatever day we arranged next week.

We hadn't met each other's friends. I was pretty sure he hadn't told many people about me. People were still getting used to the idea of him being separated, I'd justify to myself. It was a small town – it was understandable. But occasionally something would crop up and he'd have to cancel, and it would be two weeks before we'd see each other. Then there was no sense of urgency or excitement or, in retrospect, effort when those meetings finally happened. He was still sorting things out; there was a lot to work out about the kids. He was having a rough time. I needed to be patient and understanding. I tried to be there for him as much as I could and to keep anything I was going through to myself … Yeah, it's okay. I hear it too.

It's hard not to flinch rereading it. There's *plenty* in my extensive dating history to cringe about but this, I guess, relationship makes me flinch and urge, *Come on, Claire*. I want to go back to 2018 me and hug her, then shake her and point out all the blind spots that she felt but couldn't necessarily see. I want to tell her that she doesn't have to make herself smaller, her needs smaller, just because he was more able to express and assert his. She didn't have to feel grateful just because she liked him and he liked her, that, actually, she deserved more. I now get the frustration my sisters and friends felt at the time.

Three months later and nothing really had changed. We had been seeing each other for five months, and while the time passed quickly, I think I knew, given the feeling in my gut and how much headspace it was taking up, this wasn't going anywhere.

And I liked him, quite a lot actually. When he was there, when he was present, he was lovely. Warm, affectionate, funny and we had a lot of craic together and genuine chats. I found him ridiculously sexy and I almost didn't dare to believe it when he reciprocated the interest. He was different to guys I had dated before. But I could see the imbalance. I could see how much I was facilitating him, as well as how much I was diminishing my own needs and expectations. I guess that's growth in itself … but it still didn't make it any less painful. I liked him. I liked the idea of him, of us. This was the closest thing I'd come to having a relationship in years. It was so close to, but at the same time so far from, what I wanted for myself.

It wasn't just Darragh: it was work, the expending of energy in building someone else's dream. I was giving hours to the puppet theatre but it looked like it might close in September. That would be a big source of income gone – but so much more than that.

Yet amid all this, something so joyful, so pure happened. Something that had me boxing off the confusion, unrest and, at times, sadness I felt. I wasn't denying them but now they had to learn to coexist, to share the spotlight with a new set of feelings: joy, pride and heart-bursting love. In early May, Robbie Dowling was born. I would never in a million years have anticipated how emotional that day was. My sister, my little sister, had had a baby. My parents had their first grandchild. Matt was a starry-eyed, tiny-Leinster-rugby-jersey-buying uncle and Sarah and I were proud aunties. The next day we all were bundles of emotion, not knowing what to do with ourselves as we watched the clock and counted down the minutes until visiting hours.

I couldn't walk but had to do that weird hop–skip walk that is just that little bit faster but more socially acceptable than the full-on running my body wanted to do up the hospital corridor. Lying in the bed, hair scraped back into a ponytail and face pale, Katie looked tired but 10 years younger. I couldn't wait to see my new nephew. But more than anything I wanted to wrap my arms around my sister, tell her how proud I was of her and how much I loved her. Picking up baby Robbie, my future godson, I told him how much he was loved.

There's so much emotion around the birth of a baby – thankfully, in my family's experience, it was utterly joyful. But it also pulled things into perspective. What was I doing 'tipping away', to use his phrase, with a guy that, five months in, wouldn't meet anyone in my life.

Holding Rob in my arms, I knew that this was something I wanted some day.

I thought back to a time on Utila, when I was 34. Beyond Utila, in the vague some-other-time's-problem future, I knew I wanted a family. But this lifestyle of no make-up and a smattering of freckles lent itself to my being more ambiguous about my age. Yes at 34, I felt the pressure of my biological clock, probably more than I did in my late 30s, and while it wasn't out of the question, having a child when I hadn't met someone seemed like a far-away goal with a whole load of steps missing in between. That year I'd managed to put all of those thoughts out of my head, adopting a younger persona. I passed as late-twenties, and with that gentle fudging of the truth I could easily assure myself, *I've loads of time.*

Rewinding the clock, my new age took the pressure off to the point that I actually believed it.

Getting ready to return to Ireland from Utila, I sat on a sun lounger digging a makeshift beer holder in the sand with my feet. I love the feeling of pushing through the soft, dry sand to find the cooler wet sand below. At home, you don't have to do that for very long. On Utila, I had to burrow through inches of powdery white sand that trickled through my toes as it would through an hourglass. The water that was a sparkling blue during the day was a blanket of black with only the waves that barely reached our feet breaking its cover and revealing the gossamer clear water. My friend, Claudia, and I sipped our beers and had the conversations that fit so well into these settings. These conversations spoke of our hopes, our wishes for ourselves that we sometimes barely dared say to aloud. Claudia was a German freediver I'd become close to during the previous few months. She was efficient and punctual, in keeping with the German stereotype, but had a heart of gold and an endearing sense of humour to go with it. We'd be going our separate ways in a matter of weeks after a full-on, intense eight months of sharing our lives. We've kept in touch and, like many of the people I met 'on the move' or through freediving, she holds a special place with me. Claudia was a good friend.

'Do you want to meet someone? Settle down?' I ventured. It's not like we hadn't had that conversation 100 times before. We'd flirted with and speculated about and even dated guys that had come through the school we were staying at. We talked at length about men and the relationships that had shaped us for better or worse. We were both living on a backpacker island in the Caribbean – there can't have been too many that had worked out!

But there was a change in the air, maybe just for me. A sense of back-to-school, maybe, moving on but unsure of the next step.

'Sure, but not yet.'

'Yeah, me neither.'

I don't think I even had the awareness to cross my fingers behind my back. I don't think I fully believed myself. We were soon joined by an older couple, Steve and Linda. They had come through the dive school a few months earlier and were a favourite among the long-term residents. Both on their second marriage, they were mellow and adventurous and seemed to have a knack for living and enjoying the moment. Sometimes interruptions to those kinds of conversations are unwanted, the addition of a new person or people changing the dynamic and bursting the bubble of intimacy and vulnerability. Not with Linda and Steve. We continued chatting, their perspective and wisdom a welcome contribution.

'Oh, girls, to be young again and free. Enjoy every minute.'

'How "young" do you think we are, as a matter of curiosity?'

'Oh! Late twenties?'

'We're 32 and 34,' I said, pointing to Claudia and myself respectively.

'Oh. That's a little bit different. Would you like to have children?'

I nodded quietly, taken aback by her candour.

'If I could offer one piece of advice, don't leave it too late. If you know that's something you want, don't bury your head in the sand out here, figuratively or literally.'

And my bubble burst.

It was perhaps the most refreshing dose of reality I've ever received. It named the strange time-pressure I'd felt but didn't know how to deal with so I'd just ignored it and hoped it would go away.

Staying with Darragh felt like a form of head in the sand. I'd moved forward with that promise to myself, not to be ashamed of what I wanted and to be more honest with myself in setting out to get it. It's not like I wanted a child now or even particularly with him. But I didn't want to stay put for another five months, head in the sand, things looking exactly the same. I wanted more. I felt I deserved a little bit more.

But decisions are never that clear-cut, not for me anyway. Messy, merging, and no sooner have I laid out my reasoning that I know in my gut to be right than the galloping horses of *I don't know, maybe I'm not – maybe this is just how it works* trample all over it.

My brain was noisy and rebutting every argument it put forward a second later. My thoughts were pulled in different directions and my emotions followed suit.

I had to get out. I had to get away. I knew what I had promised myself: that this year would be different. I would stay put, and I'd find a way through. But I couldn't think straight and I began to feel more and more raw.

Maybe if I didn't go for long? Maybe if it was less fleeing-the-scene and more of an early summer holiday? That felt more normal, a holiday. People with jobs and houses and responsibilities go on holiday.

But I didn't want to do two weeks beside a pool in a resort. I wanted to go underwater. I needed to clear my head and let my needs float up to the surface instead of hosting a relentless back-and-forth debate inside my head. I needed to *not* think, but just be.

That very sentence seems like the equation that for me equalled one thing: freediving.

So in May 2018 I went back to Dahab.

chapter 8

FEAR

It's time to introduce you to a really big character in this book. Perhaps I've mentioned them, their name popping up here and there, but they warrant a proper introduction. This is someone who has been by my side the whole time; they're never far away, particularly during the big or landmark events in my life. Even when they're not around, I feel their presence, their influence. They give me a funny feeling in my stomach, quicken my breathing and play with the speed of my heartbeat. At times they even stop me in my tracks.

Dear readers, meet Fear. It's remiss of me not to have properly introduced you sooner. Perhaps you already know them? They're the kind of person you don't remember meeting for the first time – you've just always known them; they've always just ...

been around. Like taking a photo and later spotting someone in the background that you recognise. *I didn't even realise they were there that day!*

Maybe right now you're shuffling through memories wondering, *Do I know them? Did I meet them back when ...?* I can understand your confusion. Fear is a skilled shapeshifter; they can disguise themselves as a dull ache in the pit of your stomach. They can lift the hairs on the back of your neck and pebble-dash your skin with goosebumps like a masterful conductor. That jittery feeling before a deadline that draws your hand closer and closer to smacking the self-destruct button? Fear. The impulse to shout at your unsuspecting partner insisting that *you're fine* in a tone that maybe hints at something different? Fear.

They're the person that follows you on Instagram, watches all your stories. They remind you that they're there, they're watching, with the seemingly innocuous comment under a post that has you frowning at your screen and hours later wondering, *What exactly did they mean by that?*

Fear is a conversation starter, a mischievous voice that whispers in your ear, *Who do you think you are? Discuss.* And then retreats to watch the outcome, only stirring to stoke the fire at the most inappropriate of times.

Somewhat ironically, Fear is fearless. Guileful and unafraid of reaching out, putting themselves out there and collaborating with different emotions, they are capable of building a spiderweb network of contacts that stretches far beyond themselves, insidious, and can always reach you in some way or another.

As familiar as I am with them, it sometimes takes me a while to recognise Fear. Have you ever seen someone in the distance, their gait looking vaguely familiar, so you squint and squint, but it isn't until they're embarrassingly close to you that you exclaim, 'Jesus, 'tis yourself!'

Fear always manages to slip by the doorman, unnoticed, even still.

But they have a few distinguishing features that are their tell.

It starts with me wanting to switch off. Nothing out of the ordinary there – I've mentioned many times how I decompress. But with Fear the difference is subtle, often starting as one thing before transitioning imperceptibly to another. Instead of switching off, I'm actually trying to numb. I feel discomfort or overwhelming tiredness. I have a drink to unwind. Doesn't matter that it's a school night, it's just one glass. Sure, it's practically medicinal. Silent prayers are whispered and I thank the universe for placing me in Ireland where there are so many opportunities to excuse and facilitate having a drink. Also one is never one. One is like ticking your age box on an application form: 35–39, I fall somewhere in that category. If you have one drink, you'd tick a 1–3 box and fall somewhere between.

And then there's always one for the road, but in this case the road is the hallway from the sitting room to your bedroom. It's not the healthiest way of dealing with the discomfort.

Years of cognitive behavioural therapy (CBT) and dialectical behavioural therapy (DBT) courses and hours upon hours of counselling have left me well equipped with definitions I can pull out when the moment calls for it. Coping behaviour: doing something to change how you feel. Yeah, this definitely falls into the negative-coping-behaviour category, but the internal justification debate in my head rolls their eyes and counters, *It's only one drink, for feck's sake.*

Probably doesn't take a genius to figure out how that one works out.

I do the same with food. I fill myself with comfort foods in uncomfortable quantities. It's actually not as easy as you would think. You need to switch off, disengage, to eat that amount, to push through the discomfort and keep going. Lifting the fork to your mouth but trying to keep your eyes averted from the heaped plate of beige below you. Thoughts of *I'll start tomorrow* appease the notifications going off in my head reminding me of whatever diet I'd started three days earlier. Tomorrow sounds like a good day, a good idea. Always hypothetical, tomorrow is the best day to redress the ever-growing imbalance.

Next up is distraction. This is probably my favourite and (casually flicks hair over shoulder) where I really come into my own. There's the small scale, the beginners league. I've a deadline due? No worries, I'll just straighten my hair first. Done. Wait, I can't possibly start with my eyebrows looking like this. While I'm at it I may as well paint my nails. Just to be clear, this girl has, on many occasions, pulled up the legs of her pyjamas so they don't peek out from the end of her dryrobe, split her stripy-socked toes with flip-flops and pottered around to the shop, hair in a messy knot on the top of her head, pulling the whole look together with the addition of giant sunglasses, whatever the weather. I am never more groomed than when I am at home on my own and have something important that I am trying to put off.

Isn't that just procrastination? a heckler yells from the gallery.

Ladies and gentlemen, this might look like procrastination but underneath I think you'll find (as I rip off their mask, *Scooby-Doo* style) ... Aha! I knew it. It was Fear all along.

From there I take it up a level: spinning in all directions, I frantically search for somewhere to redirect my attention. How this manifests depends on the stage I'm in. Sometimes I exercise a lot. It takes over, the physical demand pushing down other sensations. Easier to focus on stiff, achy muscles than disquieting agitation, the root cause you can't quite put your finger on. Easier to deal with the tangible. If I go to the gym and expose myself to the torture of Bulgarian split squats, I will feel discomfort in my legs and bum tomorrow. It's a simple and explainable equation, comforting in its reliability.

Other times I work, but don't be fooled into thinking that this is an intentional use of time and energy. Invariably the work or project is for someone else – someone else's business, empire or bigger dream. I put myself at their disposal, problem-solving and anticipating challenges. The more I do, the more that's expected, and suddenly I'm fielding calls at all hours, any day of the week, the idea of being on the clock long gone out the window, shopping for birthday cards and filling out car insurance forms because my writing is neater. I've gone from trying to go above and beyond in my job to becoming a personal assistant.

It's never tackling a project that will nudge me towards my own goals but that I've put on the long finger. Don't be silly! There's a high chance that *very idea* is the sneaky little feck that called Fear in the first place, inviting them over to hang out, have a coffee and a catch up. It will be work that is a diversion, often kind and sometimes above and beyond but, ultimately, not a smart use of resources. But because it ticks the box of work, I can let it slide.

I have missed so many deadlines and applications for projects that I'd love to do – jobs, theatre bursaries, research and speaking opportunities – love and would be terrified of at the same time. I start off by downloading the application; I sometimes even go so far as to print it out. Scanning the required criteria my stomach clenches and I feel my thoughts shutting down, turning in on themselves. I shove the forms under a stack of papers on my desk and play along with the charade that I'll come back to it later … if I'm not too busy.

Sure enough, the deadline will draw nearer and I'll take it out for another cursory look. The essay-style questions seem far beyond my capabilities. A short bio? But I don't have one, and assembling my random work to form something akin to a CV just makes me feel … ashamed, embarrassed, inadequate. I probably don't have enough experience for it/maybe the timing just isn't right/I probably wouldn't get it anyway, I rationalise, savouring the instant relief of not having to put this information together, not having to put myself out there, and at the exact same time, feeling disappointed in myself that I'm once again retreating, falling at this hurdle.

Back in Leaving Cert preparation days, I would head up the stairs, detailing what I was going to do in this study session. Mum would call out after me, 'Remember, you can fool me, you can fool your teachers, but you can't fool yourself.'

With each passed deadline, with each opportunity I let slide, my excuses and justifications wear more and more thin. I am not fooling myself any more. I know I am just afraid.

Fear makes your world feel smaller. Fear manipulates you into *making* your world smaller, drawing your boundaries closer and closer to you, relying on rigid control to make sure you're operating well within the perimeters of your comfort zone. And it is just that: comfortable, like a well-kitted-out, plush velvet cage. Not much room to stretch or explore but it sure is comfy when you're sitting down ... Until you notice that this luxurious little cage isn't very well ventilated. Actually, it's getting pretty stuffy in here now that you mention it. Your breathing has to accommodate your new environment by stretching up on its tippy toes from being low in your belly to reach and lift your clavicles with each short, shallow breath.

It's fine if I just don't (gasp) *stretch out* (exhale). *Maybe* (gasp) *if I lie down* (exhale). *Yeah, that feels* (gasp) *better* (exhale). *I just need to* (gasp) *lie still* (exhale). *There* (gasp, exhale).

Fear locks you into a state like a remote-control car that is running out of battery: it's working, but just *not quite* as it should be. Erratic, never settling at one speed, clunky switches in direction until it comes to a shuddering halt and then something has to be changed.

I've reached that point, that halt, many times.

Here's the thing about Fear, though. Dealing with them once doesn't ensure you've obliterated them for good. It seems that life creates opportunities to confront Fear again and again, in all its forms.

Fear is a phoenix. You can watch them burn a thousand times and still they will return.

When I teach people the fundamental skill of free-diving, holding your breath underwater, I ask them to push up their sleeves and watch whatever bit of technology adorns their wrists.

Cold and without preparation I ask, 'Okay, hold your breath for as long as you can.'

Most last 35 to 40 seconds before they gasp, red faced. Anyone that lasts longer with a passive expression on their face, I raise my eyebrow at knowingly. Letting sneaky bits of air out your nose doesn't count.

Afterwards I ask them what made them take a breath.

'I felt like I was suffocating.'

'I needed to breathe.'

'I was running out of oxygen.'

'I had a sudden urge to breathe.'

All reactions are heightened at best and explosive in the extreme: the fear of running out of oxygen and the body tensing against the sensations, the heat in your face, the involuntary movement of your intercostal muscles that pulls your diaphragm up underneath your ribcage. I won't fib, it's definitely uncomfortable and can be an intense sensation when you first experience it.

Then we get into it. I explain how long I can hold my breath for, not as a casual brag but to show there's so much more beyond those initial feelings of discomfort and so much you can do to adapt your reaction to the discomfort. That discomfort, that urge to breathe is not actually you 'running out' of oxygen but a build-up of CO_2. How much we can tolerate varies from person to person. You can prolong its arrival considerably and you can build up your tolerance, but the real skill and take away in a breathhold is to soften your reaction to the discomfort, physical and mental.

Fear is a little bit like CO_2. It is, at best, a little uncomfortable and, at worst, pulls your head back, eyes wide, body rigid, gasping for air. Where you fall on that spectrum often depends on you. Fear is a broad spectrum, and different situations will warrant different reactions, but like I've said, it's also a shape-shifter, it'll lay low and send in doubt or self-sabotage to do their dirty work, watching the carnage from a distance like a smug, assured puppet master.

But like those urges to breathe during the rise in CO_2 on a dive, freedivers need Fear. Let's take the discipline of static apnea, lying flat on the surface of the water, airways submerged. Measured in time, this will typically be your longest breathhold. Without moving or, as the name suggests, lying static, it's the most energy efficient ... well, physically anyway! The urge to breathe and rising CO_2 are pieces of information, cues to assess how you're doing, how relaxed you are, and opportunities to soften and reframe the experience. They're lessons in observation without judgement, creating a pause before reactions and resilience. If each time I identified Fear in me as the underpinning emotion and viewed it as an opportunity for even one of these three, there would be considerably less angst, overthinking and anxiety.

The temptation on a breathhold would be to eliminate CO_2 altogether. It certainly would make our breathhold more physically comfortable, but it would also eliminate a whole series of important information points. It tells us how we're doing, what we might need to adjust; it gives us clues and reminders and allows us to assess our progress and how far we can push ourselves. Without CO_2, we get none of that. We either have enough oxygen or we don't; we've eliminated a whole dialogue, a complete feedback loop. How that looks in freediving is that we are conscious or we black out, light on, light off.

I've done (and do) so much to remove, eradicate Fear from my life. I've mislabelled them, called them by a different name and put a bandage over the wrong wound. I've exhausted myself swimming against the current but desperate to be always on the move: *if I don't stay still, Fear can't catch me*. I've eaten and drunk my way around it, anaesthetising its effects. I have locked the door, pulled my curtains and hid under my bed, pretending not to be home, when Fear came knocking.

Little Claire, Little Claire, let me come in!

No, not by the hairs on my chinny-chin-chin.

And sure enough, Fear always manages to huff and puff and blow my house in.

Each time Fear and I come face to face, there's an element of relief. I can see them for who they are, not the myriad of emotions, thoughts and experiences I've tried to pin the blame on.

It's not that the recognition makes it easier, it just helps me to move through to the next phase: dealing with it. Think of a scary movie, the building of tension, the music that's twisting every one of your nerves into a tight knot: you almost *want* the killer to jump out and get it over and done with; you can't handle the fraught anticipation any more. Once it's over, the story can move on.

Always a slightly surprised 'mouth-forming-the-shape-of-an-O' realisation – I can't believe I didn't realise it, recognise it sooner: I'm just afraid. And, yes, the word 'just' belies the effect Fear has had on my body and mind, but that's so much easier, or maybe purer, than the self-flagellation I've indulged in, body twisting and writhing with each lash.

I'm just afraid.

The remote-control car has finally come to that shuddering halt and now something has to be changed and the car set in a new direction.

Like I said, I've stumbled to this halt many times but none more so than the second half of 2018. I'd returned from a brief second trip to Dahab and tried to settle back in, do things differently. But by autumn, I felt like I was suffocating in the smallness of my surroundings and unable to tolerate the unbearable discomfort of living my life. Something had to change.

Anything.

chapter 9

NOTHING CHANGES IF NOTHING CHANGES

Summer of 2018 and my family were getting ready to sell my granny's house where I'd been living. It was a leap that needed to be made and I immersed myself in the full-time job of trying to find rented accommodation. I went to view a room in a little house in Wicklow on a sunny day in mid-July. It was in a house nestled under the trees and beside a river. All it needed was birds and woodland creatures to wake me up in the morning and help me dress. It was, in a word, idyllic. I sent out a silent prayer to my granny, thanking her for helping me to find it. I felt at sea: I needed to find a stable base so I could build on the other elements in my life. The rent was reasonable. It was quiet. It almost seemed too good to be true … 'Thank you,' I whispered and just as quickly chuckled at the notion of her hearing, rolling her eyes and scoffing at such sentimentality.

Flags went up from day one, move-in day. I parked around the back, using the back door to move my belongings into my bedroom on the ground floor. The landlords, a couple, were pottering around the kitchen and very ... at home. I closed the door to my room and sat on the new mattress still in its plastic.

Each time I moved into a new place I always felt a bit uneasy – bare shelves, a new environment and locale to learn: it was normal to feel unsettled. But this felt different. Maybe they were just finishing cleaning, about to head off and leave the new tenants, myself and a woman called Heather, to it at any minute. I ventured out and gave them the benefit of the doubt. After a tour of the house and a list of the house rules, which included the instruction 'we don't eat in the sitting room', my fears were not assuaged. *We?* Their daughter lived on the top floor in a self-contained flat – we just shared the entrance. They brought their daughter down to meet me and left us in the kitchen, exiting after saying, 'Now, we'll leave the three of ye to make friends.'

We? Make friends? I felt like we were children pushed together by our mothers and told to play. What the *fuck* was going on?

Heather, must have caught my expression. I'd only met her moments earlier, but in that instant we shared a moment of alarmed confusion.

Oh God, I think I've really misunderstood things.

My spidey senses were tingling and my idyll seemed to be slipping away with each second that passed.

Gut feelings are seldom wrong. This wasn't a straightforward house-share. The boundaries were blurred and the house was often like a train station – people we didn't know coming in and out at early hours of the morning and throughout the day. Everyone who has lived in a house-share will have stories of quirky characters and living habits. I am certain that I'm one of them for other people. But this situation wasn't quirky or in the 'ah sure, you have to laugh' category. It was a family trying to facilitate their adult daughter living on her own and bringing in people to possibly fill a role that straddled friend/carer. The funny thing was, Heather and I had both worked in care work or therapeutic settings. That made us both pretty determined to be able to draw our boundaries and have a home in which to remove those hats from our heads.

It was the first place I'd rented and lived in after a few years of boomeranging back to my family home. I wanted a stable base. I wanted somewhere I could have people over for dinner, maybe even have an adult sleepover. I definitely wasn't going to be doing that in my childhood bedroom or the box room in my granny's old house. I wanted to ... feel my age, I suppose. My sister and friends now had houses of their own and I felt stuck as a perpetual crashing-on-the-couch character, though, in my mid-30s, I had long since outgrown it.

This place was a start. A huge compromise in autonomy even as a renter, but it was a start. Hidden away in this village in Wicklow, I had a chance to put things down, process, plan and just be myself. I wanted my life to be more intentional. I wanted work that fulfilled me and helped me to fund freediving plans that weren't always made last minute as an act of desperation to glue together a sense of self that was falling apart. I wanted to steady my feet, to build my sense of self into something more robust. I wanted to thrive but knew I'd have to nurture and tend to things carefully first. This house was the space and the time I needed.

Another bright spot in this weird little set-up was being thrown into it with Heather. Heather was the type of person where you look forward to hearing her keys rattle in the front door. You knew within minutes she'd be landing on the couch opposite you, cup of tea in her hand, declaring, 'Well, girl ...' and from there you'd swap stories of your day, lament the soggy bottoms on *Great British Bake Off* or generally pass time long after the intended 'I must head down to bed' declaration.

Talking to her was easy. There was a shared experience of being women in our 30s to 40s, navigating dating life that had largely moved online and unsure about how to finally have a house free of landlords. She got it. With her, I didn't need to launch into the justifying and over-explaining that I felt I had to do with others.

'But sure, I'd love to be free and single.'

My ability to give something other than a caustic response to this glib refrain that I often heard had long since evaporated. Heather understood the yearning. She also understood that wanting to share your life, your adventures, with someone didn't mean you'd settle for anyone, that you could feel lonely but, at the same time, cherish your independence. She understood that one set of circumstances didn't negate the moments of joy, spontaneity and divilment that you welcomed in your day-to-day life. Her use of language and ability to encapsulate any situation in the simplest of language always amazed me. She was a straight talker but never brutal. She always had words to make me feel better – even if it was her acknowledging there was nothing she could say to make things better.

Heather would have been *just* a really great person, an incredible listener and general wise gal if it wasn't for her wicked, wicked humour. She went from absolutely ridiculous to full-on zany, peppered with that dark humour that makes me rub my hands in glee. Like having a dark, black coffee with an incredibly rich, decadent chocolate cake, something that cuts through the sweetness yet ties it all together. That was Heather.

There weren't many dates during my time in Wicklow (so much for adult sleepovers). I had broken up with Darragh shortly after I returned from Dahab at the end of May. We hadn't seen each other for weeks. A friend suggested that Darragh might surprise me and pick me up at the airport. 'Maybe,' I replied, but I knew better. We broke up the following week. A part of me knew it was the right thing, but another part was heartbroken by the lost potential, real or imagined. Months later, I was still licking my wounds and needed to assess what I was looking for and how to avoid that situation again. I guess my head just wasn't up to it.

In late October, I was muddling along with work and making an effort to get back to a level of fitness and give myself a bit of routine and structure. One evening, I headed out for a late 5K run. From our house in the village, I ran up a winding lane, huffing and puffing up the hill it covered, dodging cracks and bumps in the path that had previously sent me sprawling. It was dark. I loved it. At the top, the trees to my left gave way to show the mountains in the distance. Bathed in moonlight, they looked eerie and otherworldly. Gaps in the trees overhead revealed a starry sky. It was one of those perfect autumn evenings, cold and crisp, the smell of winter on its way. There was nothing exceptional about the run. I used the torch on my phone to light the way in front of me. Yes, there's a part of me now shaking my head and thinking, *Jesus, Claire! Running on a dark secluded avenue ... are you taking the piss?* I naively hadn't given it much thought. I felt like being on my own and I loved that view. But no, it's not something I would do now.

I did a few laps around the little park opposite our house to round it out to a full 5K and headed on in. *Yeow*, my calf felt a bit achy. I was heading away on my cousin Lynne's hen weekend the next day. My other cousins were in the late stages of training for the Dublin Marathon. I didn't want to be the one hobbling around after a measly 5K run so I wrapped an ice pack in a towel and grabbed my plate to head upstairs to the sitting room to eat my dinner (yes, we *do* eat in there!) and rest my leg for a few minutes.

The next day, my sisters and my mum were driving up to Carlingford for the festivities. *Jesus, my leg feels really sore.* It felt hot and stingy, like a really bad razor burn. There was a raw red mark on my leg where the ice pack had been. I'd covered it in aloe vera that morning but it was throbbing. I unbuttoned my jeans and pulled them down to my ankles. I'd do the journey in my knickers and let my leg breathe. That evening, though somewhat numbed by endless rounds of Prosecco, I went up to change and have a look at my leg.

JESUS CHRIST!

The back of my calf had erupted in angry-looking bubbles that were excruciating to touch. I washed down painkillers with another Prosecco and got back to the matter at hand. They got worse and worse. I had difficulty bending my leg, and that night I propped it up with pillows, unable to put any weight on it. The bubbles had filled with fluid and started to discolour – yeah, this wasn't normal. I picked up my car from Leixlip the next day and headed straight to the hospital. Cellulitis was mentioned more than a few times. They used a purple marker to outline the parameters and got to the job of 'deroofing' the blisters.

I haven't experienced anything like it. I felt like my skin had been scorched and they were scraping nerves. I couldn't put weight on my leg, let alone drive. Heather and a friend came to pick me up and drive my car home. I crawled into bed, shook and gritting my teeth at the pain that left my whole leg swollen and rigid.

I returned to the hospital the next day. A new doctor took a cursory look at it, declared it wasn't cellulitis (but didn't offer an alternative), scoffed at my lack of pain tolerance, slapped a new dressing on and, with an almost 'you'll be grand' attitude, sent me on my way. 'Yeah but how long do I keep it covered for?' Nope, he was gone.

I got myself home and fell face down onto the bed and slept for the next 24 hours.

A few days passed. I hobbled from my bed, taking my time up the eight steps to the sitting room, arriving onto the couch drenched in cold sweat. I was going to have to change the dressing myself soon. I limped up to the chemist for supplies – I couldn't put it off any longer. I had started to bleed through the dressing. I tried to describe to the chemist what I needed without actually *knowing* what I needed. I must have been garbling because the chemist kindly sat me down and gave me a glass of water.

'How about I have a look and we can go from there?'

We unwrapped the dressing, and as we got to the

last layer she recoiled. 'Who did this? Did you do this yourself?' I explained I'd been to the emergency room. 'You need to get this seen immediately. Go straight to St James's Hospital and ask to be seen by the burns unit.'

I didn't quite know why I had to go the burns unit but her urgency took me by surprise, as well as bringing tears to my eyes. It was so painful.

The treatment in the other hospital had left me open to infection and exacerbated the wound. So I made my first journey to St James's. I later learned that I had gotten an ice burn as a result of a faulty icepack. Through the towel I'd wrapped it in, and my running leggings, I'd managed to 'burn' my leg quite badly. They brought me back every day for a week, then every second day for another two as they treated my leg.

No one likes being injured. It's never on anyone's to do list. Not being able to move around took a toll on my mood. Running and exercising were out the window, two big feel-good factors, and driving was to be kept to a minimum. I felt cut off and isolated and utterly sorry for myself. By the first few days of November, the frustration and pain had slipped into something a little darker. The tired, draggy feeling in my joints and behind my eyes was perhaps started by, but had now evolved past having anything to do with, my injury. It wasn't just a fed-upness but a weariness. I'd been doing this cycle for years and I just didn't feel like I could lift myself out of it again. This time last year I had been competing in freediving, setting national records. The contrast was stark and I just didn't know how or have the energy to get back to being that girl.

I was tired, tired of explaining or justifying how and why I sometimes felt like this. Tired of fighting or having to prove myself against the perceptions of weakness that the word 'depression' sometimes elicits from people. I felt like I was falling between the cracks, not for the first time. All I wanted was to retreat further and isolate … but I knew that was the last thing I should do.

♦ ♦ ♦

The call came the first Sunday evening in November. I was in Leixlip making a massaman curry for my family. I know that sounds strange to someone who has never experienced depression – to feel depressed one minute and be cooking for a group the next. That's part of it, I suppose, and one of the reasons I think it's so confusing for people on the outside looking in, trying to understand and help. I knew I had sunk pretty low. I also knew it was time to reach out, or at the very least put myself among people who loved me. Cooking dinner gave me something to focus on and helped with any nervous energy.

I saw the missed calls on my phone.

'Just in Leixlip having dinner. Everything okay?' I replied by text.

The phone rang again immediately. I held it up to my ear with one hand while stirring in peanuts with another. My friend, Brita, had died.

Brita's story is not mine to tell. It is her mum's. It is her partner's. I always feel strange talking about it, let alone writing it. It feels enough to say that Brita was loved by so, so many and is missed by more. Her death showed me how far the effect of one good person can spread into the world. In the days before her funeral I learned more about her work, the volunteer programmes she'd quietly taken part in and even set up. I thought I knew my friend but I was astounded and humbled by the amount she had done in her almost 36 years.

Grief is a funny thing. It touches us in different ways and it seems no two people's journeys cover the same path, let alone the same timeline. Grief handed me over to Fear. I was completely at its mercy. For months, I used to check the timestamp on my family's WhatsApp. Matthew had gone on a night out? I'd check to make sure he'd been online the next morning, looking for clues that he'd got home safely. Sarah was flying home from London? I'd check to make sure the flight had landed and, again, waited to see her online. Dad had a cold? He *needed* to go to the doctor and get it checked out. All of them, my parents, my sisters, my brother, my brothers-in-law and my nephew, I want to pull them in tightly to me and protect them, keep them safe.

And I thought back to that morning in my bedroom on the day Brita died.

I had moved around my room getting dressed, killing time before my mum picked me up to bring me to Leixlip. I needed to get out of the house, go anywhere, eat breakfast in a café, anything to move myself physically out of this moment. Depression shrouded me like a thick black cloak.

I threw on clothes and caught myself in the mirror.

I can't do this any more.

To this day I can't remember what exactly I meant by that.

I can't do this any more.

What did I *mean*? I was hardly planning ... No, I know I wasn't. But I knew I couldn't do this. But do *what*?

I hammered out permutations of this conversation with myself. I needed to resolve it to alleviate the guilt. I needed to make sense of it, scan it for clues and context so I could try to reframe it. I saw all that Brita had been denied. Gulping anguished sobs late into the night, I thought about all that lay in front of her that had been extinguished in one day. Still, for me, all I felt was hollow.

I spent days on the couch. I got through my birthday, which was a couple of days after her funeral. The day sickened me – how are you supposed to celebrate? The charade of blowing out candles and making a wish was just too much of a tall order. I lived in pyjamas, ignoring the increasing collection of tea stains that they were accumulating.

Like a photograph, I remember the moment something shifted.

I can see grey tracksuit bottoms, my tears splashing down onto them. There are crisp wrappers at my feet, beside two cups that have been there since ... yesterday? The day before? One foot has a striped slipper sock on and the other is bare. Maybe I couldn't find the other one and had abandoned the search. Maybe one foot got hot and the other didn't – that sometimes happens. I see the legs of the wrought iron table that I'd pulled around to hold my breakfast, lunch and dinner plates. I felt utterly alone and completely pathetic. I wanted to peel my skin off and start all over again; this one was just too uncomfortable.

'I can't do this any more,' I repeated. 'Something has to change.'

I needed a project. I needed a Big Project, something that would give me structure to move, however slowly, forward, that would carry me through the last few weeks of the year and set me up for the new one. A project that would not only require me to develop my physical wellness, but my mental wellness too. I needed a project bigger than me that would require me to push the walls back and expand my living space, coax me outside into a world that is wide open. A world that is full of opportunities for growth and development and, most of all, living. Living, not existing. I needed a project, an injection of passion to remind, or maybe prove to, myself that I was capable of living a life much bigger, much fuller and on my terms.

Have you ever tried googling such projects? There's no one-stop page with a list of suggestions and a filter feature where you add your details and requirements and tailor the results to your situation. Age, living situation, finances, easy enough to fill out. Now, where's the 'inject meaning into your life' box? Sure, there are bucket-list suggestions but many involve grabbing a backpack and heading travelling. I am never averse to doing that – I'm a big fan of it, in fact. Selling my car, anything that was worth something (so probably *not* my car) and heading off. Going somewhere and freediving was usually my answer to this. But I was physically unfit and emotionally … well, banjaxed. Freediving is a sport that requires just as much of you mentally as it does physically. I had a lot of work to do to get back to a baseline before freediving was an option. But more than that, I felt that this time it wasn't what I needed. It would merely be a plaster – an incredible plaster, but a plaster all the same. I'd spent the last few years heading off, and each time I returned, I was hit with the sense of displacement; I didn't know where I fit in. I knew I needed a new way of coping, something that was an investment in my future rather than fleeing as a way of passing time in the present. Getting on a plane and meeting new people, experiencing new ways of living, had undoubtedly broadened my mind and created space for me to breathe, but now I needed a change that would translate to living in Ireland as well.

So you can see, it's a pretty tall order for any project.

Congratulations, Big Project, you've been selected as the successful candidate. You will bring me out of this grief/despondency/depression and build me up to be a shinier version of myself while ensuring that I don't arrive at this juncture again in the near future.

I'm relying on you so … No pressure!

It sounds like one of those 'what could possibly go wrong?' situations.

Everything: the answer is everything could go wrong by putting all your eggs in one Big Project basket.

I remember listening to a podcast that described the opposite of depression as being, not happiness, but meaning. I think I was looking for meaning at that point. I'm really good at all-out, big, extreme, all-encompassing projects that take over your life and consume every waking moment. They suit my 'all or nothing' personality perfectly. But I knew that that was, in a way, almost the same as heading off. It would come back to bite me months later.

This unicorn of a project needed to nurture my mental well-being as much as it would make demands of my physical well-being, something that would include other pillars of health: sleep, food, stress levels – all the boring, non-instant-gratification stuff.

I started with a half-marathon. Googling running events I came across the Wicklow half-marathon that would take place the following March. Perfect! That would give me four months to get in shape, train and nail it. I texted Katie and put it to her. She was in! James would even do it too. Brilliant! I started filling in the online application while my head got to work on a training plan. I jumped up to grab my credit card to pay for my slot ... and promptly fell over, smashing into the couch opposite.

My leg. How in God's name had I forgotten about my leg? What sort of glitch had happened in my brain that I had completely overlooked the fact that my right leg still couldn't bear weight? Absolute gobshite!

'Kate? I probably won't be able to do the half-marathon. I sort of forgot about my leg.'

'Yeah, I was wondering! No bother, we'll do it anyway. Maybe you can mind Robbie?'

Right, small false start. Back to the drawing board.

With this setback, I returned to freediving, looking at images, casually starting to put dates into websites of airlines. I was just looking – I knew it wasn't the right thing but that didn't mean I couldn't window-shop for a little while. Falling further and further into an online freediving rabbit hole, I learned that the World Championships were taking place in September 2019 in Nice.

That'd be a cool thing to be part of, I mused idly.

Wait a minute ...

The idea came less as a lightbulb moment but more as an old lightbulb in an abandoned house. Maybe a lightbulb in an attic that hasn't been used for years. You pull the string and the air crackles with the sound of electricity before the light flickers on, casting an eerie glow onto the shadows beyond.

It was ten months away – that wasn't going somewhere at the drop of a hat. That gave me time to prepare, time to work on my fitness and a structure in which to build myself, all of myself, back up again. It was taking that flee-to-freedive instinct and updating it, adding elements that might make the results more long-lasting.

I floated the idea to Heather, outlining what I'd need to do to get there.

'I don't know freediving or the significance of the World Championships – they mean nothing to me. What I'd be interested in is the work you'd have to do to get yourself there, the skills you'd equip yourself with. I presume they're ones that are transferable and will benefit you beyond the competition? The process is the part that intrigues me.'

'Ugh, don't give me that "it's not the destination, it's the journey" bullshit.'

But she was right.

Tossing in my bed that night, I mulled it over. The 'journey' that I'd rolled my eyes at was exactly what I needed, but the thought was laced with more fear than I'd confronted in a long time.

I probably wouldn't be eligible anyway.

That's right, Claire Bear, shut that shit down.

I hadn't been in the water for ages either. I'd have

so much training to do, both physically and mentally.

So much training. You've probably forgotten how to freedive altogether.

And it'd be so expensive. I didn't have that sort of money.

Too much money, you'd be broke. Do you really want to invest every penny into this?

Plus I wasn't a deep diver. What would people think?

Exactly. I'm glad you said it, not me.

The project would require me to put myself out there, me – not a company I worked for, not someone else's dream, me – in a way I hadn't before. It would leave me exposed, vulnerable and open to judgement and criticism that before would have paralysed me. I back-and-forthed in my head. I heard all the thoughts shutting it down. Angry and indignant, they made their case, presented valid arguments, but this time, something inside me was still curious. Something had shifted. Ramming my fingers in my (mental) ears, I ignored the thoughts and hammered out an email to the organisers. I'd just see if it was possible first. It probably wasn't but then at least I'd have tried. I hit send not quite knowing the response I was hoping for.

I thought back to a picture taken on top of the Blue Hole, the tricolour high above my head. I wanted a moment like that again. I wanted that smile, a face without a screed of make-up that glows from within. I looked happy, but more importantly, I looked proud of myself. I wanted to be proud of myself. Maybe that's something I had neglected, forgotten how to do: the ability to acknowledge achievements big or small. To feel a sense of pride in progress in all its forms. Like a muscle not regularly flexed, it had become weak and flabby. With excessive focus on the *should*s I had abandoned the *maybe*s, the *sure why not*s, the sense of playful curiosity. In that moment, such a stark contrast to the imagined image, I wanted to meet myself where I was, with no pretence, no pressure and no judgement. I felt the overwhelming urge to take myself by the hand and guide myself along to a place, a state where my smile tilted my head back, chin towards the sky, and I felt proud of myself, my achievements and this funny little life I was living.

That moment, that image was so rich, so quickly filled out by my imagination, that I could feel the heat of the sun, the giddiness in my fingertips, my cheeks twitching involuntarily, unable to hide my smile, my eyes sparkling and full of life, my shoulders back and down, my heart out and open to the world around me. It was with that image that my thoughts went from black and white to all colour.

The very prospect shook me to my core.

Hello. Fear, I thought you'd be stopping by. Actually, I need your help …

Standing side by side with Fear, our eyes fixed on exactly the same point, it was then I decided that that was exactly what I would set out to do.

chapter 10

COUNTDOWN

January 2019 hit a little differently. Don't get me wrong, it still felt double the length of any of the previous months. Our sitting room in Wicklow still felt stark and bare once we'd taken down the Christmas tree and decorations. But I didn't feel as rudderless. Still raw, still testing out the sound of my plan, not to mention my leg, with all the steadiness of a baby who's learning to walk – but at least I had a plan. The whole endeavour seemed huge, overwhelming but memories of those long dark nights in November had narrowed my focus. I refused to let the bigger picture engulf me and instead, I decided to tackle eating the elephant the only way I knew how: one bite at a time.

The World Championships ran from 7 to 14 September. I would need to be there a week or so before to get some dives in and settle myself. Before that, I would have to train in depth, and Dahab was my best bet. It was where I knew, I felt comfortable and I could get coaching. I would need at least two months, and even that was cutting it fine.

Working backwards, I aimed to leave Ireland at the end of May. The very thought gave me butterflies and I couldn't even go there in terms of arriving at the World Championships!

One thing at a time. The first few months of the year, all I had to do was work on my fitness. I had started with a personal trainer named Keith, who guided me through workouts that took into account my injured leg. Between him and a physio, I slowly became able to do more. At the same time, I also wanted to change my approach to rest. I wanted to find a way of resting that was more restorative, more soothing than simply switching off in front of a screen. I didn't want to necessarily shut down, but to gently sit with any feelings that arose in my body with no distractions.

I dealt with the months that were immediately ahead of me and trusted that the work of each quarter of the year would build me up and carry me into the next.

♦ ♦ ♦

3 January, journal entry – 20 weeks until Dahab
I booked a load of sessions with Keith today. One part of my brain is freaking out about money but the other part knows that if I want to

get back into the gym, into my body, I'm going to need help. I think he can help me. He's also a form of accountability. Meet him at 4 p.m. or forgo the session and waste money. That should put a fire under my arse.

8 January – 19 weeks until Dahab

Sweet mother of God, I hurt. My legs hurt. My arms hurt. Walking hurts, bending hurts, fecking blinking practically hurts. Well, at least that means I've started!

22 January – 17 weeks until Dahab

Feels like an 'emotional hangover' sort of day. I couldn't sleep last night and that's when all the thoughts creep in. I'm tired. I feel lonely. Those two are a jump-up-and-down sort of invitation for old demons to revisit.

As long as we are rejecting ourselves and causing harm to our bodies and minds, there's no point in talking about love and accepting others. (Thich Nhat Hanh)

You know what you have to do, Claire.

What does 'being kind to myself' look like at the moment? What little things can you do tomorrow that builds a little bit of trust within yourself? What does being a friend to yourself mean to you? Because you can be a fucking deadly friend …

10 February – 14 weeks until Dahab

There's something unsettling me this evening. I can't quite put my finger on it.

I'm sifting through stuff that's cropped up over the last day or two but none are quite hitting the spot.

I feel like I'm running my hands over my skin, looking for the place of tenderness, pressing old bruises to see if they're the source of the niggling discomfort.

Nope.

Hey there, Feeling of Unease,

I promise to give you some space if a bit of time is what you need. I promise I won't drown you in alcohol or suffocate you in food. I'm happy to check in with you for a moment if that would help?

During yoga this evening I got that feeling again, that I need to do more. Not load more gym sessions into my timetable, but give more space to my body, to my breath. There's answers there that I've been covering up with Netflix, food, drink, men. I've forced them into hiding where they now lie dormant.

But they're stirring.

I can feel you, I can hear you, I am willing to create a space, to listen, to accept ... let me know when you are ready.

4 March – 11 weeks until Dahab

I went up the Sugar Loaf with Katie today. I love that stage of getting fitter when you don't count that as your exercise for the day. It's just a walk and a chance to catch up. Gym is going well and today I really could feel the work paying off. Aesthetics and shape are … well, problematic and complicated but I realised today that I really value that, I suppose, freedom in my body. Want to go up the Sugar Loaf? Sure, I've the gym first but I'll meet you this afternoon. It's a really nice marker. Okay I won't lie and say I don't care about my weight or how I look but skipping up the Sugar Loaf today I felt (dare I say) proud?

25 March – 8 weeks until Dahab

Yesterday was the Wicklow half-marathon. I'm cracking up at the idea that I wanted to run it! Kate and James did it and I used the time to push Robbie around the 10K course. Sure we'd a lovely stroll and chats! I used that voucher I had for Druids Glen, the one I got but didn't use with Darragh. After lunch Katie headed off for a massage, and James and I sat and chatted while Rob crawled and climbed over and between the two of us. James has such a clear way of looking at things. I've been holding back on booking flights to Dahab. I know I need to get into the water to train. My sessions with Keith are great at building my general fitness, I can do breathhold sessions in my bed and try to calm the fuck down in yoga, but I need to get into the water. There's something that's holding me back. Maybe booking it makes it real? James said something today that really hit home with me: 'You have to just go for it, just go all in. You'll regret it if you don't. We're all behind you.'

So simple, encouragement and support … and he's right. I'll regret it if I don't.

So after a night in the hotel with Kate, a lovely dinner and a swim this morning, I came home …

And booked my flight. I guess I'm doing this!

3 April – 7 weeks until Dahab

If you don't plant in the spring,

You will not reap in the autumn.

This is your time to move forward, but remember, you're already doing that. You are taking steps, making conscious decisions to move forward. Future Claire is going to be feckin' thrilled!

Of course you're going to be tested; old habits are seductive bastards. They want you back but you need to remind yourself they no longer serve you.

Progress is like a pendulum. Maybe every bit of the backswing is as important as the forward. You're still making progress: keep the focus.

16 April – 5 weeks until Dahab

Warning! Imposter! Imposter Alert!

Ah, lads, I'm shitting it. I'm so scared. I don't know if it's fear or just being hit in the face with the imposter stick. I don't look like an athlete, I'm not going to be diving the depths of the other athletes, who the fuck do I think I am putting myself out there for this?!

Don't be distracted looking left and right. What other people are doing is none of your business. You're not competing against them, you know that. Stop spending your energy speculating. People will think or not. Who cares? You've no control over that. At. All.

You're grappling for the self-destruct button – how well has that ever worked for you before? It's a short-term relief but you'd be negating so much work you've ALREADY DONE. Keep her goin', Patsy.

17 April – 5 weeks until Dahab

I spoke to Heather today. She doesn't get freediving so my 'but I'm not deep enough' fears fell on deaf ears. In her straight-to-the-point way of looking at things she reminded me that it's not the destination, it's the journey (in all its clichéd glory), and that the journey has already been the 'making of me'.

28 April – 3 weeks until Dahab

I CANNOT FUCKING BELIEVE IT. I got a sponsor! There is someone who wants to give me money towards this mad trip. How the hell has this happened?! Jesus, I can't believe it.

Timewise Systems are going to sponsor me to go to the World Championships. One of the girls from aerial silks class, her husband Ronan owns a company and she put me in touch with him about potential sponsorship. I met with him today, and he's agreed! I can't fecking believe it! It's absolutely incredible! It's a mixture of relief and pressure and back to relief. This is a game changer! I think it'll take a few days to sink in. Aaaaargh!!!

1 May – 3 weeks until Dahab

I leave in 23 days. Today a major spanner was thrown in the works: we got our marching orders from the house. I can't believe it ... well, I can. It's kind of right on brand for this place. Still, I'm spinning a bit. A big part of this plan was to have somewhere to return to. I didn't bank on having to pack everything up and then potentially go back to Mum and Dad's once I got home from the World Championships. That's why this trip was going to be different. I'd be returning to a place of (relative) stability. Fuck. I did not factor in having to pack up in my preparations. Jesus, this will be the ninth move in eight years. I've so much to finish up before I go – this was the last thing I needed.

13 May – 10 days until Dahab

I'm scrambling. I'm against the clock. Late nights, packing boxes. Living in chaos. This isn't how I wanted to be heading away. It's funny, as soon as they told us to leave, we were both done with the house. It looked the same but suddenly it wasn't our home. I don't want to be here. I just need to get it all sorted, realistically put it into Mum and Dad's, and then forget about it. Yeah, it'll definitely save me money on rent over the summer. There's a part of me that rages at them, how they've done and dealt with things, but there's another part that feels like it's another part in the jigsaw, untethering me from this place, this time ... and maybe all that's gone before. Who knows? There's a high probability I'm drunk on tiredness and just talking shite.

18 May – 5 days until Dahab

Tonight is a full moon and my last night in Wicklow. It feels apt. I headed up the Sugar Loaf just after sunset and watched Dublin light up from the top. I can't believe I've been here for nine months. It's flown by but I was a different person when I moved in here last August. There hasn't been a boyfriend to share my bed here like I had hoped … but tonight, looking out to Dublin, to the sea, I told him I was ready for him. I wondered what he was doing, told him to keep on going, that we'd meet soon. It's silly, but I need to talk to him, I need to tell myself he's out there, and until we meet, I'll be doing my own thing. This crazy, terrifying but 'fuck it, I'm doing it' thing.

20 May – 3 days until Dahab

Goodbye, Wicklow, thank you. It was a refuge, a haven during a really difficult and unsettled time. The best thing that came with the house was Heather. I'd have been lost without her. She truly has been a source of light this past while. I hope I find a place next October, somewhere with a little bit more security. Somewhere I can welcome visitors. Somewhere with clear boundaries and a cool, kind and respectful housemate to share it with. Oh, and it has to have space for a gigantic Christmas tree! But for now, so long, Wicklow. Thank you.

23 May – 0 days until Dahab!

… and I'm off!!!

I'm sitting here in Departures, a coffee beside me and my fins at my feet. That was some sprint to the finish line. Every time people ask me if I am excited to go, I can never quite tap into it. Until this very moment. I've packed, unpacked and packed again, got to the airport, got through security and there's nothing but an overenthusiastic bunch of queuers between me and my flight!

What I'm doing is right for me – I can feel it in every part of me. This is the right way forward. I know it because since I've made the decision, things have lined up, even fallen into my lap. Just look at the sponsorship money. Never in a million years would I have dreamt of that. Thank you Timewise Systems. Even the situation with the house. No, it wasn't pleasant and I definitely could have done without it but, like I think I said before, it's like it has released me completely to focus on the next few months and opened me up to the possibilities beyond!

Last night I did a meditation (I know, the notions on me!). A phrase came into my head that repeated over and over.

I'm ready when you are.

Over and over again.

Ready for what ...?

Anything.

chapter 11

PAUSE

Wearing my beloved Bosco T-shirt ... 30 years before I went to work with Bosco's family!

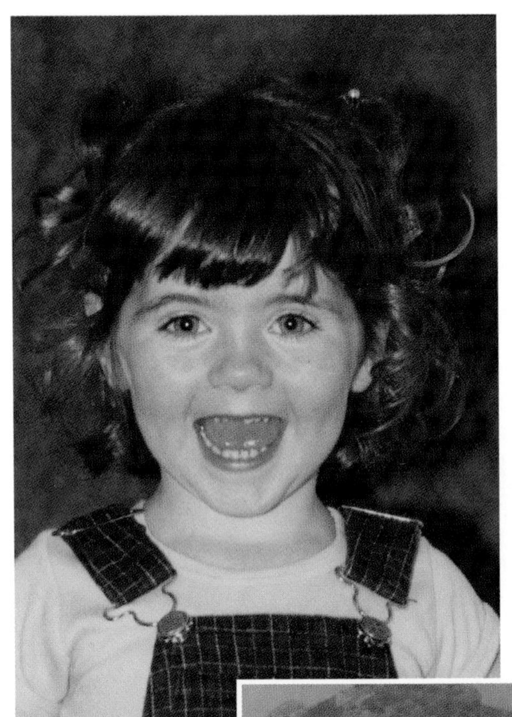

Me, aged 2. (God, I used to love those dungarees!)

Did your swimming togs have a belt?

Bicycle shorts, baseball caps and bumbags: looking stylish in Disneyland.

Left to right: Matt, me, Katie, Sarah and Dad, on our summer holidays in Kilmuckeridge, Co. Wexford, in 1994.

An obligatory awkward confirmation photo with Katie, Matt and Sarah.

Mum and Dad, forty years married. Clare, 2021.

An Chlann. Left to right: Sarah, Katie, Dad, Mum and Matt.

Laura and I behind the scenes at the Lambert Puppet Theatre.

Playing with seals in the Galapagos. (*Jesse DuBois*)

Below the surface. Ras Mohammed, 2022. (*Mark Tilley*)

First national record! The Blue Hole, Dahab, 2017.

Putting on your wetsuit is the hardest part of the dive. Aqua Marina, Dahab, 2019.

So far out of my comfort zone! Photo taken during the 'magical light' hour in Dahab in 2019. (*Janna El Borno*)

A typical day in the Blue Hole. Dahab, 2019.

A new buddy.
Dahab, 2019.

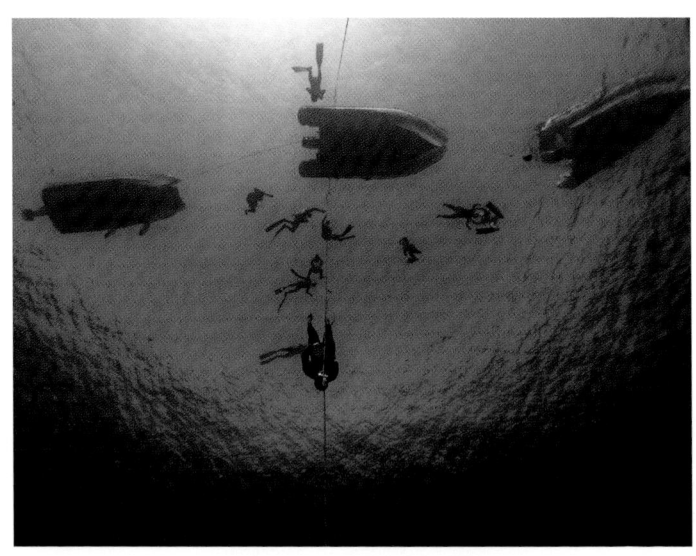

Down the line. Cyprus, 2019. (*Daan Verhoeven*)

Nathan and I after the last dive of the World Championships in 2019.

Towards the light. Cyprus, 2019. (*Daan Verhoeven*)

Back to cold water. Greystones, 2020. (*Niall Meehan*)

Niall and I on the last day of Freezbrury, 2020.

Lockdown swims. Bray, 2020. (*Niall Meehan*)

Back to the cove in Greystones. (*Niall Meehan*)

I'm back! Dahab, 2020. (*Huub Waaldijk*)

Return to the water. Ras Mohammed, 2022. (*Mark Tilley*)

Playtime in Shark Observatory. (*Mark Tilley*)

The next adventure. (*John Gillooley*)

New adventures. (*Nanna Kreutzmann*)

What is a pause?

A pause is a stop.

Why do we pause?

We pause to take a breath, to make sense and to emphasise meaning.

Every year while we were in school, my sisters and I revised our speech and drama theory for our annual exams. Every year we got out our well-marked, dog-eared notes and started revising and relearning everything from why we pause to the rhythmic scansion of iambic pentameter. We quizzed each other, imitating our potential examiners. Our age groups and grades dictated different requirements but we always started out together from the same point, the beginning: the pause. What is it and why do we do it?

Recently I spoke to my sister and she said the word 'pause'. Thirty years later it still triggered the recitation of a question and an answer. Thirty years later we can't say the word 'pause' without reciting its definition and function. It's that embedded into the library of family vocabulary, shorthand and in-jokes.

For the next few days after speaking to my sister those four lines segued in and out of my internal soundtrack. I paid them no more attention than I did James Blunt's 'Goodbye My Lover', which had somehow also wangled its way in there. I have no idea why but I find it's best not to question these things.

I went about my day, my tasks and my to-do lists accompanied by this bizarre remix. Day-to-day life: scrolling, writing, updates, news, tags, alerts, texts and beeps. Moving distractedly from one piece of technology, from one form of media, to another, never fully present with any one thing. To-do lists reeled through my head while I mentally ran through ingredients for that night's dinner and at the same time replayed a conversation I had the day before that had been niggling at me since. None of these were high-stress items but together they formed a cumulative hum, a building of energy that left me lying in bed, exhausted and drained ... but wide awake.

Wide awake and confused as to why sleep hadn't arrived immediately. I'd spent the best part of the day fighting it off. I'd yearned for the moment my head would hit the pillow and I could finally switch off. Yet there I was, muscles tensed against the mattress in my quiet bedroom while in my head sentences and songs wove and overlapped to form a tortuous ear worm, its words dancing on the backs of my eyelids like a demented karaoke machine.

What is a pause? (Goodbye, my lover.) A pause is a stop. (Goodbye my friend.)

Why do we pause? (You have been the one.) We pause to take a breath, to make sense and to emphasise a point. (You have been the one for me.)

I needed to press pause. I needed to take a breath. I needed some respite from relentless noise, chatter and assault on my brain. I wanted to rest. I wanted to relax and unfurl this ball of tension that seemed to have settled in my tummy.

Placing my hands on my belly, I rubbed them back and forth, reassuring, giving my body a tactile cue and coaxing my breath lower into my body. Desperate to pull myself from the whirlpool of thoughts in my head, I drew on sensations in my body. The solidness of the mattress beneath me. The weight of the duvet that created a cocoon of warmth around me. The smell of my moisturiser. The sound of wind outside. Running through this sensory inventory averted the rising panic. Feeling my belly push my hands away with the inhale, things started to slow down.

In, two, three, four, pause. Out, two, three, four, five, six, seven, eight, pause.

In, two, three, four …

My hand twitched to involuntarily conduct, to keep time with this soothing rhythm. My eyes closed and I let myself be carried by this anchoring cadence, this lullaby of air. Reassuring in its reliability, I drifted off, promising myself to pause more tomorrow.

Life, unchecked, felt full of busyness. Too much hurry, too much stress. Too many machines vying for my attention. Too much caffeine. Too much tension. Too many expectations to move, to make, to do, to achieve. Too many words, thoughts. Too many emotions, each as crucial and compelling as the next. Too many stories.

What is a breath?

A breath is a stop.

Why do we take a breath?

We take a breath to pause, to make sense and to point sense.

A simple inversion of this oft-repeated phrase was not quite a 'Eureka' moment, but more like finally being able to reach an itch that had been bothering me for days, a 'that's the spot' moment, a quietening of the brain, a sigh of relief. Locked into the routine of everyday life, how often do we pause? How often do we take a breath? We breathe approximately 22,000 times a day. How many of them are conscious efforts to create a pause, to create a space where we attempt to curb that momentum, where we let our bodies unfurl their tight grip and release the tension we're holding? We'll plough through tasks, breathing to function, but how often do we pause, breathing to nourish?

Just take a deep breath ...

It sounds so simple, so obvious. A solution to all problems. Think about it – how many times have you been told to do this?

Stressed? Just take a deep breath.

Nervous? Just take a deep breath.

Back pain? Just take a deep breath.

About to speak? Just take a deep breath.

At the doctor? Just ... you get the picture.

I'm guilty of it myself. Standing in front of my choir, a group of 50 singers of varying ages, abilities and experience, I have said calmly: 'And take a deep breath.'

The result is usually I watch 50 pairs of shoulders lift up to the ceiling with their eyebrows, more often than not, following suit. The effect is one of startled anticipation. 'STOP!' I shout at the widened eyes. 'Breathe, for the love of God!'

Trickles of laughter dispel the tension that filled the room upon this collective gasp.

Just take a deep breath: such a simple instruction with apparently more potent healing powers than Sudocrem and a cup of tea combined. Why is it so hard?

We know how to do this – we were born doing it. Lying on our backs, arms stretched over our heads, thumbs tucked under our fingers in protective fists, our bellies rose and fell with each inhale and exhale.

And then life happens; the muscles in our chest develop. Our habitual posture shapes our body. We develop tension; muscles tighten while others compensate. Our experiences start tweaking how we present ourselves. Our environment and beliefs take up residency, leaving their mark, locking us into an idea or aesthetic of what our bodies should look like and what we must strive for to be considered 'normal' or 'beautiful'.

Trauma, each interaction, how and when we should show emotion. The technology we layer into our lives that keeps us constantly stimulated and locked into a state of pseudo-alertness. So many elements criss-cross and overlap creating a feedback loop to our brain, bending, restricting and limiting our body's most intuitive movement.

Whether it's in shallow gasps or tension-filled sighs, we move so far away from those simple, pure breaths we took as babies.

So if we breathe approximately 22,000 times a day, that's 22,000 opportunities every day to compound the bad habits we've learned, inherited or developed over the years. It is caused by exposure to constant stress, but even when it's removed the poor breathing patterns remain. We don't need to be told to just take a deep breath: we need to be shown how to do it.

So let's pause and take a breath to nourish.

Sitting where you are, lean your back against the chair behind you. Forget about the schoolteacher instruction of sitting up straight – right now we're going to aim for a combination of lengthening our spines but maintaining a softness. Relax the line across your chest that runs from one shoulder to another. If they fall forward and round a little bit, that's okay. Softness. Start to take a breath in through your nose and focus on keeping the top part of your chest soft and relaxed. Now exhale making an emphatic *ha ha ha* sound. If you end up laughing, whether through amusement or self-consciousness, that's a bonus! With this specific warm-up, you're waking up, engaging your diaphragm and letting your body know where this breath is going to take place. Place your hands just below your belly, and when you breathe in, let your belly gently push your hands outwards, slow and controlled.

Next you're going to exhale for double the amount of time; so in for four, out for eight, this time keeping the stream of air slow, steady and controlled. Does this feel strange? Don't panic. Think of the 21,999 other times you've done a version of this today, a different way. It'll take little while to override the old habits.

So we practise.

I use music – 'I Giorni' by Ludovico Einaudi to be precise – 5 minutes and 59 seconds of music (incidentally, the same amount of time I can hold my breath) that soothes me, distracts me just enough to let go of the narratives that have filled my day. Sitting on the floor, cross-legged, I breathe. I reward myself with this time, this pause. Feeling my belly gently move with each breath, I try to stay with the sensations in my body. The cold of the floor on my bare feet, the softness of the blanket around my shoulders, I send my attention all around my body.

Feeling the softness of my belly, my sides, I gently guide myself away from remarking upon it, from attaching a judgement to it. This moment is about nourishing, not admonishing. Like a Russian doll, the breath holds another pause within itself, a moment of suspension between the inhale and the exhale. This pause, this subcategory, is the breathhold: apnea, or the temporary cessation of breathing. Just as I need oxygen to fuel my lungs, I need breathhold to test my strength, to sharpen my resilience and to eke out a way of finding softness and relaxation amid stress and discomfort. Here, my thoughts no longer pull me along with them but pass in front of my eyes, allowing me to observe with a benign curiosity, like looking out the window of a train. This is a space where I'm stripped bare. No phones, no distractions, I'm forced into the moment with all its sensations, discomfort and starkness. I can resist and struggle against it or I can find a way through. I can find a way to meet myself, break down the disconnect between body and mind and lean into this space of honesty that our day-to-day rarely affords us. This is what breath and breathhold mean to me – it is my way to stop: stop overthinking, stop holding myself back and stop difficult and uncomfortable emotions from taking over. I breathe to pause, to be in that moment, to make sense and to see sense.

Each slow, deep breath pulls me down from the surface of day-to-day living, of fake-it-till-you-make-it, of expectations and judgements, and lulls me into the quietness of a more honest, more compassionate and more reliable self.

chapter 12

THE TURTLE AND THE HARE

Opening the door of my bedroom the first morning back in Dahab in almost a year, I looked at my home for the summer. My apartment was already flooded with light and being warmed by the morning sun. I opened the door to my balcony, which I wouldn't close until I left. Over the tops of buildings and palm trees, I could see the Red Sea and, beyond that, the mountains of Saudi Arabia. My feet did a little dance on the hot tiles, my bum a wiggle of happiness, and I wanted to fist pump the air. This space was all mine, no one else's. It was calm, it was bright, and any nerves I had about the next phase of the plan were assuaged by the fact that I had a beautiful base to do it from.

Wriggling into my wetsuit, I nearly dislocated my shoulder and put my back out.

Heading down to the entrance of the Blue Hole, I looped back twice to pick up pieces of equipment I'd forgotten. Hobbling across the rocks to the water, *Don't slip don't slip don't slip don't slip don't slip.*

Putting on my fins, my head slipped below water. *ARGH!* I'd forgotten to put my snorkel in my mouth. I spluttered and turned the snorkel upside down first, this time emptying it of water before trying to breathe through it. This was mortifying.

Athlete my arse, I thought as I made my way over to the buoy.

Everything felt clumsy. My wetsuit felt tight. I wiggled my toes in my fins, my feet becoming reaccustomed to the foot pockets. How had I done this before? Was this part always this hard?

I'd like to say that once I had slowed down my breathing, had time to mentally place myself in the Blue Hole again, taken my big breath and pulled myself down into the blue that all that changed ...

Of course it didn't. In fact, it couldn't have been further from the truth. My body and brain, having spent 12 months on land, were shouting, *What in God's name are you doing, woman?*

I knew they had been no ordinary months, but here I was. I was rebuilding and presenting myself, ready to get reacquainted with freediving and life underwater. Vulnerable but determined, I had no answer for them other than to reassure them. *We're grand. We'll remember. Just give us all time.*

Three months to train for the World Championships wasn't a lot of time. Most athletes had been training for the whole year, starting with base training in their own countries before arriving in Dahab for adaptation to depth and working on their respective disciplines. I had a lot to cram in but I knew none of it would work without patience.

The process of adapting to depth, even adapting to being back in the water, is slow. I think I'm naturally more hare than tortoise: I'll leg it at the start but you're likely to find me asleep just before the finish line. I was so excited to be back, so determined, so eager to go, go, *go*!

But I know a slower pace allows me to remember the sensations, learn to fully relax and let go, quieten my mind and, most importantly, allow the body to adapt safely. More 'slowly and steadily' instead of 'quickly and carelessly'.

To bring home the 'more tortoise, less hare' analogy, in that first session I wanted to drop the line another 5 metres *just to see*. Putting my face in the water, there she was: a beautiful turtle cruising by our line. Paying us no heed, she slowly and steadily swam by and over the saddle of the Blue Hole out into open water. Right. Message received. Slow it is.

The days fell into a pattern quite quickly. My alarm clock went off at 6 a.m. and I wandered out to my living space, never getting bored of the light that greeted me like a warm hug. It was clichéd and cheesy but I couldn't help it. I hit play and the sounds of Bill Withers' 'Lovely Day' flowed from my speaker. Dancing in my knickers and whatever Disney tank top I'd worn to bed (thanks, Penney's!), I clicked on the kettle for a cup of tea (mint, I'd save my caffeine for after diving) and rolled out my yoga mat. 'Proud Mary' saw me through the start of my stretching routine and from there might go into the *Blues Brothers* soundtrack or maybe the *Commitments* if I was feeling homesick. Waking my body up in the sunshine while belting out the words to my favourite songs became a routine that had this not-usually-an-early-bird girl hopping from her bed in contentment the minute the alarm went off.

Afterwards, I did some short breathholds and lung stretches and finished off my time on the mat with a short meditation. Journaling was the last part of my routine. I used to set two minutes on a timer and scribble whatever thoughts or worries or expectations were in my head that day. Sometimes I was scribbling right up until the last second; other times I was writing, 'I've nothing left to say, I just want to go diving!' But each morning I would try to write, to leave behind the contents of my often-busy head with a promise that I would return to them later on, *after* my time underwater. A quick check of my dive equipment and a generous application of sun cream, and I would hurry down the stairs to make my way to the Blue Hole.

Mornings were spent diving. Nathan, my coach, picked me up in a taxi at eight and we talked through our plan for the session, what we would be focusing on that day once we arrived in Aqua Marina. I had all my stretching done so I passed the time sipping ginger and lemon tea and watching other divers prepare and carry out the bizarre looking pre-dive rituals that we barely batted an eyelid at. Still, freedive theatre never failed to entertain me.

After a session, the first port of call was always a nap or, at the very least, a lie down in the air conditioning. I resisted the urge to fling my bag down and promise to deal with it later, instead carrying it straight into the bathroom where I'd rinse my wetsuit, fins and equipment of the salt water and get them out to dry. If the colours I associated with Dahab were bright and sandy-red, the smell had to be neoprene – wet and sometimes pee-smelling neoprene. It wasn't all glamour!

Afternoons were spent meeting people for coffee and games of backgammon. Dahab was getting quieter, with people leaving for Europe or elsewhere to avoid the blistering summer heat.

'July and August are brutal,' I was warned.

I'd see how I'd fare.

Most of all I was grateful for this time. I had September on my mind, the World Championships, the competition dives. Instead of twisting myself in knots about it, I assured myself that by the time it came around I'd have learned what I needed to deal with it. I had to have some faith in the next few months.

So I took them seriously. I stuck to a routine before diving that woke me up, stretched out my body and quieted my mind. Bed time was *early*, even by freediver standards. I read a lot that summer. I'd settle into bed at 8.30 and read, lights out by 9.30 and up again at 6.

I savoured this light and airy space, a third-floor apartment all to myself. I hadn't had the opportunity to live on my own for a long time, but rents in Dahab afforded me the luxury.

Above all, I was so grateful for the time. I was so grateful to myself for taking on the challenge and not only for doing everything I could to set myself up for success but to take pleasure and pride in the process leading up to it.

My diving had changed. In retrospect, that's not surprising, I hadn't been in the water for over a year, and even at that, my last trip to Dahab had been dominated by what had been going on at home – in a word, Darragh. I had been distracted and unable to find that relaxation that's so important before diving. I couldn't come down out of my head and into my body to pay attention to what was going on underwater. Racing thoughts and raw emotions manifested in physical tension, and my diving had been curtailed completely.

I was aware that I probably still carried a lot of what had happened over the last 12 months with me, but I felt like I was more honest about it, honest with myself. Instead of trying to numb or distract from it, I had worked on repairing the relationship, the bridge between my body and mind so that I could travel between, exist in both.

I began our sessions determined, focused but still, perhaps, held something inside me closed as a just-in-case line of defence. I was diving proficiently but something was off; neither I nor Nathan could put our fingers on it.

'Maybe we need to look at your relaxation beforehand.'

That didn't feel like it but we needed to attempt to problem-solve.

It wasn't my relaxation. My diving felt almost mechanical – technically fine but there was something missing. I was holding something back.

I remember the dive when that changed.

It was a normal morning in the Blue Hole, no different to the morning before. I had slept well and participated in my morning stretch-concert with gusto. I felt good getting into the water and was looking forward to the session.

I was focusing on free immersion, the discipline where you pull yourself down the line. The first part of the dive was going well. Today my ears felt good. I made the smallest of adjustments to my jaw, which meant I could open my eustachian tubes and equalise as I pulled myself down into the Blue Hole. I checked my body for tension as I entered freefall, softening my knees and letting my feet trail loosely, enjoying the sensation of the water that rushed around them. I wasn't thinking of anything, not

Will I make the depth?

How much further is there until touchdown?

I hope Nathan doesn't think that I'm a shit diver.

Am I stupid to try to go to the World Championships?

I was on the dive, in each moment as it passed. No thoughts, no judgements, no negative talk to derail me from my underwater journey.

Touchdown. Turn … and I started pulling myself up with nothing in my awareness other than the rhythm of each stroke.

I had just started to open the palm of my hand against the line and let my glide take me towards the surface. Below me and to my right was the Arch, in front of me a wall of coral. The light was flickering against the coral that were becoming more vibrant the nearer I got to the surface.

But all I wanted to do was close my eyes. I didn't want anything to distract or take me away from this feeling. In a moment that I could almost pinpoint, I felt something loosen, something unclench, like my heart space had wrestled itself from an unknowing tight grip and now was open. Free.

I felt a release and relief flooded my whole body. Only for I was underwater, I would have made a sound, an exclamation, a sigh. I don't know exactly what I had been holding onto, but with this feeling, my instinct told me it had been gently let go, released to the water around me.

I came to the surface and turned to Nathan. Shaking my head, eyes filling with tears.

'What happened?'

'I – I don't …'

I couldn't find the words. I looked into his eyes and saw a flicker of realisation, of recognition.

He reached out and, with a tenderness that surprised me, put his hand on my arm. 'Don't put it into words right now. I saw it. The main thing is, it's happened. We can talk about it later.'

He turned his attention to the other diver on the buoy and I was glad of the privacy. Swimming away, I pulled back on my mask and put my snorkel back in my mouth. Putting my face into the water, I closed my eyes, let go … and added more salt water to the Blue Hole.

After that, training gathered momentum, things clicked into place, and I found myself braver, bolder in the water. I arrived out to the buoy unapologetic: I was supposed to be there. It's not that all self-doubt had been eradicated in one fell swoop, but that moment was the reassurance I needed. It told me I was moving in the right direction.

chapter 13

HABIBI

In the late 1960s, Jacob's aired a series of ads tasked with solving the mystery of how Jacob's got the figs into the Fig Rolls. The was-he-real-or-not man of mystery Jim Figgerty was the secret-keeper, along with his sidekick Habibi. These clever ads went ... well, whatever the equivalent of 'viral' was in 1969. A generation all questioned 'How *do* Jacob's get the figs into the Fig Rolls?' Households, including my mum's, grew up repeating the catchphrase, 'Who cares, Habibi, they're gorgeous!'

And that's how this Arabic word of endearment snuck its way into a generation's consciousness and vocabulary in 1970s Ireland.

In our house, over the years, the phrase morphed into 'Who knows, Habibi?'

It became a somewhat 'Ah sure, look!' conversation closer: a discussion with no clear outcome or solution could be brought to a conclusion with shrug and a sigh and a 'Who knows, Habibi?'

My first time in Egypt, hearing *habibi,* my ears pricked up. *Wait, how do they know this word?*

I hadn't had any exposure to Arabic before this. I hadn't even known *habibi was* Arabic! Of all the languages I'd heard while travelling, Arabic was different. They were sounds rather than words and the rhythm challenged my ear as the speech washed over me. It had a completely different cadence and it was strange to not be able to pick out even one word that I could understand.

Staying in Dahab, I soon picked up *shukran,* thank you, my mouth struggling to adapt to a new way of forming sounds. It's not the most complicated pronunciation, but I didn't want it to be completely coloured by the hybrid Leixlip-Dublin accent I normally speak with. Within no time I was hearing *mashy*, a broad spectrum *okay*, after 90 per cent of interactions. I learned that if I asked the landlord if he'd be able to fix the air conditioning by Sunday and he replied with, 'Sunday/Monday, inshallah,' I had to accept I'd be living in a sweat-box for the next week at least.

And then I heard it: *habibi.* Mainly between friends, *habibi* is a greeting, a welcome, a term of endearment. Like most things, it's overused and maybe its meaning depends on its context. It wasn't until I heard it between a mother and her son that I got a sense of its true meaning. She addressed him and, though I couldn't make out many of the phrases or even see her face when she said *habibi*, I could hear that she was smiling. It's a word, a greeting, to be said to those who make you smile.

I kept notes in my phone of phrases that Ali, the owner of Aqua Marina, taught me. Before I left after my dive sessions, he'd give me a new phrase and I'd write it phonetically. I'm sure any native Arab speaker wouldn't recognise the anglicised, Claire-friendly descriptions.

Ashofak bukra – See you tomorrow.

A shoe – Okay, that's easy. A shoe, one of a pair. Got it.

Feck – Well, I'm Irish …

Bukra – Hmm, harder. Think. A springbok! Less the spring plus a 'ra'.

A shoe feck (spring) bok + ra.

Nailed it. I'll try it out on him tomorrow.

The time came and I shouted across, 'Thanks, Ali, see you tomorrow.'

No, wait! I know this … I jumped down the bays of the restaurant to grab my phone. Scrolling through the apps, scrolling … *Where is it?* Ali was looking at me puzzled. *Where the feck is it? Aha!*

'Ashofek bokra!'

'Inshallah, see you tomorrow.' His black eyes practically disappeared, his face broke into a wide, warm smile, and I couldn't help but feel a little bit delighted with myself. He was so patient – and indulgent. He made me want to practise, to get it the first time the next day.

♦ ♦ ♦

Mid-July and the heat was, as promised, brutal. I'd done eight weeks of training and they'd been full on. It's easy to overtrain and freediving puts a stress on your body unlike any other sport. I couldn't shake the tiredness even after my day off and mentally I couldn't kickstart things the way I needed to. The timing couldn't have been better – I was due to return to Ireland for a week for my sister's hen party. It would be a whirlwind trip but seeing family and friends, cuddling my nephew (if he allowed me) and eating proper food would be the break I needed before returning for the final few weeks of training before the World Championships.

Days blurred into one another. It was a whistle-stop tour of catching up with friends, some nerve-wracking radio and even television interviews, culminating in a Prosecco-fuelled celebration for Sarah, who was getting married in September. The morning after, I lifted my head from the hotel pillow ever so gingerly, assessing the damage and wondering what level of hangover I'd be subjected to. After a day of festivities, I'd called it a night at 12.30. No nightclub and sweaty dance floor for me. I was pooped and had a flight that evening.

Eight hours later I was in Dublin airport, checking the board for my flight to Sharm el Sheikh via Istanbul, buying a packet of paracetamol, a coffee and a can of Coke. I'd got away lightly. I'd seemed to escape many of the physical aspects of a hangover but the emotional hangover was in full swing. I didn't know if I needed a hug or a cry or to be surrounded by puppies or what! I was just so happy for Sarah and so proud of her and how she approached things. I typed out an overly sentimental message to my sisters before turning my phone off and switching my attention to the inflight entertainment. I needed something light, something funny. No hard-hitting drama and definitely no risking anything that could be described as 'bittersweet'. Best keep the tears to a minimum. I was a glass case of emotion and I needed the warm and fluffy. I settled on *Finding Nemo*. It was the underwater visual hug that I needed right then. I blanketed myself in my hoodie and allowed myself to be soothed by the mantra:

Just keep swimming ...

The World Championships were only six weeks away. I had three more weeks in Egypt to train and prepare and I felt lighter returning to Dahab. It had been an amazing trip. I'd spoken on national radio about freediving. I had seen footage of me diving on national news: 'Kildare woman to be the first to represent Ireland in the Freediving World Championships'. For once, my thoughts didn't cloud with *yeah, but I'm not actually a good freediver*. For once, those voices stayed silent. Seeing the Blue Hole of Dahab on the graphic screen of RTÉ's Six One news was incredibly surreal and very emotional, and I let myself sit with this feeling that I more often insist on going ten rounds with: pride. When I made the decision to compete, I knew the challenge wouldn't be the competition itself, but overcoming the self-doubt, the imposter syndrome, and putting myself forward. I watched myself and thought, *I'm doing it. I'm putting myself out there ... and it's not so bad.*

I stood a little easier in my shoes; my chin lifted a little. This is what I was doing at this moment and I was so proud of myself. It was an equally overwhelming and empowering feeling.

Add that to the festivities, the craic and the organising of a hen party that had been given the go ahead on the strict proviso of No Willy Straws, douse that whole bonfire in copious bottles of Prosecco, and that's where I was after my trip. It was wonderful but I still had dives to do. The preparation wasn't over: it was just entering a new phase and I was ready for it. My return flight had been delayed and I missed my connection. The airline put everyone who missed the flight up in a hotel on the outskirts of Istanbul. I was back in Dahab a day later than planned but my unexpected stopover in Istanbul gave my brain a chance to take a breather, and when I finally arrived back in my light-filled apartment, I was ready to go.

'Diving tomorrow, we'll pick you up at 6 a.m. It's just me, you and an Egyptian guy called Boudy.'

'Perfect, see you then.' I couldn't wait to get back in the water.

It was 31 July and the heat was full on. I had definitely acclimatised somewhat, having been there since mid-May, but standing on the road in front of my building even at 5.55 a.m., the heat was savage. My buddy, Rapha, got out of the car to greet me and helped put my gear in the boot.

'How's a' going, Rapha?' I climbed into the taxi and he filled me in on the goings on in Dahab that I'd missed. 'Who's yer man we're picking up?' I interrupted 10 minutes in. 'Oh, his name is Boudy. He's a nice guy. Quiet.' I smiled to myself. Rapha was a chatterbox so compared to him everyone was quiet!

We pulled up to the side of the road where an Egyptian lad was waiting with his gear. Wearing the unofficial Dahab uniform of shorts, T-shirt and flip-flops, only a small patch of face was visible between heavy-set eyebrows, knitted together in the middle, and an unruly black beard. He slid into the front seat, barely acknowledging us in the back, and started to talk to the driver in Arabic. He didn't look like the friendliest of people. *This will be a fun session*, I thought as I locked my eyes on the glittering blue that framed the road out to the Blue Hole.

I'd never been to the Blue Hole that early. Only a handful of other divers were quietly preparing in Aqua Marina. There was a stillness to the water; a mist hung inches from the perfect, undisturbed surface. I kicked off my flip-flops and waded in up to my knees, my eyes darting excitedly around the perimeters, drinking in this paradisiacal view. I had missed it.

It'd be a while before we got in the water to dive. There were rounds of ginger and lemon to be had, equipment to be assembled and stretching, weird breathing practices and blowing up balloons with your nose all to be done – I told you, we had some strange-looking rituals!

Aqua Marina was divided into bays. Each dive group set up in a bay, laying out their gear, cramming the table with dive computers and masks and nose clips and lanyards and equalisation tools. Not to mention wallets, sunglasses, phones, GoPros. Whoever said freediving has no equipment was fibbing. I nestled into a shaded corner, hiding from the early morning sun that had already brought the temperatures well into the 30s.

'This is a nice song,' I observed absentmindedly as I closed my eyes, leaned my head back and tried to follow the melody with my voice. Hmm, I was having a little trouble with the ornamentation.

'It's not a song.'

Opening my eyes, I spotted two small black eyes focused on me from underneath the heavy brow. The expression wasn't exactly a scowl … but it wasn't exactly *not* a scowl either.

'It's not a song, it's the Quran.'

'The –? Oh. What I was doing was pretty disrespectful then?'

'A little bit.'

'What did you say your name was again? Bodhi? Bowdy?'

'Boudy.'

'Ah right, Boudy. As in …?'

'Boudy as in Boudy.'

'Yes, of course. Boudy.'

Inward eye-roll. Jesus, this guy was tough work. But at least the eyebrow had raised somewhat and the overgrown beard had parted to reveal a smile. It was quite a nice smile, actually – it changed his demeanour completely.

In the water, I was thrilled to be back. I had no lofty goal for today's session, just to get back into it, to enjoy. Boudy surprised me by turning out to be a good buddy. He had a silly sense of humour and seemed to be going out of his way to make me laugh. The atmosphere on the buoy was light-hearted, which made for some relaxed and easy dives. It was a perfect first day back. We pulled our equipment out of the Blue Hole, giddy after the session, and worked our way back up to our bay where fruit and tea would be waiting for us.

Thinking back on it now, it was so innocent. I was 36; he was 25. Normally, I'd be glancing at him sideways, swiftly assessing if there was potential even for a little flirt. He certainly was cute, in an unkempt, overgrown hair and beard sort of way, but definitely not my type – and *waaay* too young. I appreciated his attempts at humour, but it wasn't that sharp, fast-paced, battle-to-the-death sort of Irish humour that lit a fire in my belly. The laying down the gauntlet, the sheer challenge of keeping up and possibly surpassing was what I loved in my 'flirting'. I loved the back and forth. Seeing the appreciation in their eyes at my quick ripostes. I didn't know how to look up coyly from under my eyelashes. I'm 5 foot 7 and could on occasion be described as a 'fine-sized girl', so I don't scream petite and delicate, triggering that nurturing, protective instinct in men. I don't giggle – instead it's silent laughter punctuated by an ungodly sounding snort. Attractive. But this very Irish approach to flirting was the only one I felt comfortable doing – it was the language of dating that I knew. It was fun, it was competitive and so damn attractive. Darragh had had it in spades. Our text battles had me laughing out loud in the supermarket. Stopping in the middle of an aisle to fling back a response that would hit his phone seconds after he pressed send. I could match him and I know he liked it.

Boudy didn't really have potential, even for a holiday fling. But he seemed nice, so when he suggested a game of backgammon that afternoon I thought nothing of it other than *I love backgammon and cake.* It was my favourite post-dive past-time. Oh, wait, he didn't say anything about cake ...

'Sure, how about Time café? They've a nice backgammon board, decent coffee ... and good cake.'

We played our three games of backgammon – for some reason we, and that's a much broader we, always played games of backgammon in threes. Usually that's when we'd say goodbye, part ways and go about our respective evenings.

'Do you want to go snorkelling?' he ventured.

'Now? Sure, I'll just go and grab my gear. Lighthouse?'

'Actually, there's a really nice place to snorkel up near where I live. I'd love to take you.'

Look at him go! At the time it seemed to be just figuring out the best places to see things. Both playing backgammon and heading into the water are normal Dahab activities. It wasn't until months later that I realised this was a huge thing for him to ask. He was shy and the cultural norms he grew up with didn't encourage dating.

Okay, it was late in the afternoon and I suppose a sunset snorkel could be deemed romantic but ... that was just a coincidence, right?

I grabbed my togs, snorkel and mask and we jumped in a taxi to his apartment. He finished gathering his gear and offered, 'You can get changed in there if you like,' pointing to his bedroom. 'I'll wait outside,' he added before leaving, not just the room, but his apartment.

That's a bit weird, I thought. It's not like I was mad keen to shtrip off, but I was definitely used to getting changed into swimwear in public. I've long since mastered the under-the-towel shimmy that allows you to undress while protecting your modesty ... most of the time. This gesture made me a little more self-conscious, and going into his room to get changed felt more intimate than getting changed on the shore. This was an innocent activity, but it still seemed important for him to show me respect and let me know that there were no ulterior motives to him inviting me up there. The gesture stuck with me. It's not that I thought all men were sleazy, far from it. I had plenty of male friends, particularly in Dahab, but this stood out. It was the complete opposite of the dating I'd experienced at home, where sexual innuendos and gestures were shoehorned into what could start off as and appear to be the most innocuous meetings or activities.

Putting my face in the water, all thoughts (and overthinking) left my head. The sea was barely up to my ankles but this was angry-looking sea urchin territory, so the undignified belly crawl was preferable to picking those spikey feckers out of my feet. This was my favourite time of day to be in the water. The light made everything above and below magical. We followed brightly coloured fish, spotting the undulating lion fish and gliding past clusters of sea urchins, until we reached the drop off. Allowing our legs to fall towards the sea floor, we pulled our bodies vertical and broke the suction of our masks from our faces. We took in the pinky-purple sky that framed glowing sandy-red desert mountains. On my right in the distance was Saudi Arabia, in front of me a row of desert mountains leading up to the Blue Hole. To my left and towards the shore was a silhouette of mosques and palm trees. It was perfect. Moments like this, everything else feels far away. Whatever else was or wasn't going on, I couldn't help but become a little overwhelmed at how beautiful it all was, how lucky I was to be there. I've so many mental snapshots of that area in that light that it's not difficult to recall the surroundings. But try as I might, no words, even by writers far more skilled than me, will ever capture the sense of perspective, the colours, the light, the vastness and the pure beauty of the scene.

As far as first dates go, it wasn't the worst …

To say Boudy was a delightful distraction is undoubtedly doing him a disservice. We buddied up, setting our own schedule for dive sessions. He understood and was impressed by my plan to compete in the World Championships and took on the role of unofficial coach. He happily accompanied me on my sessions, dispelling any nerves or pre-dive tension with jokes and looking out for me in a manner that I was completely unused to. With him, I got my first diving PB – personal best – in years.

The Blue Hole in the mornings, backgammon in the afternoons, and then he'd take me to try new, more traditional places to eat. He laughed at my complete inability to handle the heat and often arrived at my apartment with bottles of ice-cold water and ice-cream sandwiches from the shop below. He brought me hiking in his beloved mountains around Dahab. He hopped, skipped and jumped with ease (and in flip-flops!) along steep cliff faces while I crawled on all fours behind him. I was sweating – I'd forgotten to mention my fear of heights.

Evenings were spent on my couch, huddled over a laptop watching *Brooklyn Nine-Nine*, or simply lying on the sun loungers on my balcony looking up at the stars. I would be leaving Dahab soon for Nice and the World Championships, but I hadn't felt that relaxed in a long time. I was diving well, enjoying myself, and I felt ready.

Historically, I'd enter into a holiday romance and be dreading saying goodbye. Not this time. It's not that I was eager to leave him, but I had my sights set on September. Heading on to Villefranche, Nice, was my focus, and while I had really enjoyed his company, I wasn't going to leave Dahab after an incredible summer with heartache or anything that might distract me from my goal. Our time together was a delightful bubble spent in blue waters and under starry skies, but I saw it for what it was. I almost admired my uncharacteristic detachment. We said goodbye, I knew we would keep in touch, but for the moment I had far bigger fish to fry. It was time for the World Championships.

chapter 14

OFFICIAL TOP

The preparation for my first dive in the World Championships was a noisy one. Altogether I would be doing three dives, participating in the disciplines free immersion, constant weight and constant no fins. Many of the other athletes had come in a team, and though I knew and was friendly with a lot of them, I wished I had a companion, a teammate from Ireland. Nathan, the coach I had trained with in Dahab, was here, but he was competing. Still, it was a relief to be able to chat with him, to receive and give pep talks and generally share the experience. The competition was starting with arguably the most nerve-wracking discipline: constant no fins, or CNF. Waves smashed my face like echoey thunderclaps against my neoprene hood. The hustle of photographers, medics, safety divers, judges and officials … and most of all, my internal chatter: a constant companion, an entertainer, an ally and an enemy, they all contributed to the noise and atmosphere of tense anticipation that try as I might, I couldn't ignore.

I'd made my way to the village and answered calls from home. A text from Boudy flashed up on my phone: 'Good luck, go get 'em'. I smiled. I knew he'd be watching the live stream nervously in a few hours' time. We'd kept in touch and as a diver, he was eager to hear all the goings-on behind the scenes of the World Championships. The excitement from the previous night's opening parade had faded and I wasn't nervous, per se, but I felt emotional. It was a lot to take in. My family had come to watch me dive. Walking in the athletes' parade, carrying Robbie in my arms for part of it and holding the Irish sign above my head and the flag around my neck was a feeling I knew I would cherish for years. This new flag had been given to me by a friend and fellow Irish diver, Dave McGowan, known as McGoo to his friends. There had been a point earlier in the year when it had looked like we'd be competing together, the prospect of going as an albeit small team making the event seem far less daunting. But plans had worked against him and he magnanimously accepted it wouldn't be happening for him this year and gave me his full support instead. We'd managed to meet up when I came home from Dahab and before I headed off to Villefranche. The freediving world is small and friendships are built often on a buoy and sometimes online, without having met in person. That's how I'd got to know Dave: two divers from the same island, with a curiosity for competing and a shared love of the sport. That first coffee we shared (which was the first of many), he gave me a present.

'What is it? Ah, there was no need.'

Opening up the wrapped package to uncover the tricolour, once again I was left speechless. It was the second time someone had given me an Irish flag before heading off to a competition, and it was just as humbling and touching as before. It is, to this day, one of the best presents I've ever received.

On the day of my first dive, I got to the athletes' village and met a few male divers who had been watching the morning's dives on the big screen. The competition kicked off with women's CNF, a controversial discipline to start the competition with. So to account for first-dive nerves, I'd announced a conservative, easy dive to get the ball rolling.

'What are the conditions like?' I enquired.

'Absolute shitshow, it's been a morning of blackouts – wait, are you diving today? Sorry ...'

Breeeeeathe, Claire.

I signed in and made my way down to the boat that would take us out to the competition set-up. I was met by a French diver I had met at training the past week. French athletes have to vie for a place on a crowded team. No fins was her discipline and her one dive of the competition. Judging by her tears, it hadn't gone according to plan. I stopped to give her a hug and heard her talk of her red card through teary hiccups. Fuck, none of this was what I needed to hear. I felt bad leaving but I needed to focus on the dive ahead of me.

On the short boat journey I repeated to myself a mantra: *Smile, and fake it till you make it. Be grand.*

We arrived out to the large boat where competitors had laid out their gear and were listening to meditations and stretching. I had a little while to go before my time on the warm-up line. Not sure what else to do, I suited up and half-heartedly copied some of the other athletes' pre-diving rituals. I felt like the team from *Cool Runnings*. Like the Jamaicans at the winter Olympics, I didn't quite belong here. I was trying to emulate other teams, other athletes in an attempt to fit in ... and we know how well that worked out for them. I didn't have a coach with me. I was only diving to 30 metres. I didn't need (or deserve) a coach, surely.

'Three minutes to Official Top!'

Okay, Claire, breathe. Just take a deep breath. Relax. No big deal, it's just like any other dive ...

except that it's in the World Championships.

And you've made a big song and dance about being the first person to represent Ireland.

And it's being filmed.

And your parents are watching live.

And some of the best divers in the world are here.

And you've invested pretty much most of your savings to get here ...

But, yeah, no big deal. Just another dive.

'Two minutes!'

Did she say two minutes or one minute? Shite, I can't hear anything. Okay, come on, Claire, you've done this dive umpteen times. It's easy. It's routine. BREATHE. RELAX. **splash* *cough* *splutter* For fuck sake! How am I supposed to – *splash**

'One minute thirty seconds!'

Claire, FOCUS! *Concentrate on your breathing, Let go of tension in your body – except not too much: you need to stay up out of the swell. Christ, these waves are acting like I pissed them off in a past life. Come* ON, *Claire: at one with the water. Relax! Or at the very least, pretend to look relaxed.*

'One minute!'

One minute? Fuck this is really happening. Months of training have been building up to 1 minute 40 seconds underwater. One breath.

'Thirty seconds!'

Relaxrelaxrelaxrelaxrelaxrelax.

Fake it till you make it. You got this. One with water.

Relaxrelaxrelaxrelaxrelaxrelax.

'Twenty seconds!'

Oh Jesus! Stay relaxed. Get ready.

'Ten seconds!'

Oh shit, I can't believe I'm doing this. This is actually happening.

'Five, four, three ...'

Okay, so I'm doing this. Right.

'Two, one ...'

This is it, Claire Bear. You're doing it. Just take a deep breath and, fuck it, we'll figure out the rest as we go!

'OFFICIAL TOP!'

'Claire Walsh representing Ireland, 30 metres, no fins, national record attempt ...'

And then silence. Underwater, you don't hear anything.

I made my way down, slightly startled by the sound of and my first experience of DiveEye, an underwater camera that was recording and streaming my dive.

Block it out: just focus on the dive.

I made it down to the bottom. Nervous energy had me skip the freefall; instead, I swam all the way down. But at 30 metres, the freefall would have been the shortest section of the dive. The bottom plate arrived quicker than I expected and I reached below to take the tag. Upon turning you're allowed one pull and only within one metre of the bottom, usually marked by red tape, often referred to as the 'candy cane'. The line was bouncing in front of me in the current, and not confident I'd be able to grab the correct section, I abandoned the pull and started kicking up to the surface. I remember being met by the first safety diver and glancing towards the surface to align myself so I'd come up facing the judges.

After that I don't remember anything ...

When I think of the last part of the dive, I can't but give a silent thank you to all the time spent in Dahab, practising and repeating that particular dive. Autopilot took over and I continued my strokes, gliding up to the surface.

Friends watching the dive saw me surface. Instead of taking a few strong recovery breaths and removing my mask and signalling *okay*, I went straight for the tag in my hood. This would have been the first indicator that all was not well. It's common practice to bring a friend, or a 'coach', with you for the dive, someone to help with your set-up and coach you through your surface protocol. Sometimes, they can make all the difference. Perhaps if I'd had someone with me in the water, someone to coach me, they'd have seen this and shouted instructions – 'Breathe, Claire! Mask, signal, say you're okay' – talking me through the necessary steps to get a white card and, more importantly, stay conscious. Things might have turned out differently, but this time, I fell forward and blacked out.

Like I said before, it doesn't hurt – well, if we don't count pride. My last memory is being underwater and seeing the platform above. When I came to I was being brought out of the water by the safety team. It took me a few seconds to realise what had happened, and with the realisation came an emphatic *Ah fuuuuuuuck!*

Followed just as quickly by *What did my parents just see?*

I needed to let them know I was okay. I wanted to find a camera, to wave to them, to get out of the water and get to my phone. But my first port of call was the medical boat to be checked out and given the all-clear.

On the boat ride back to shore, I didn't know how I was going to face my family, my friends that had travelled all this way to see me dive. For many of them it was their introduction to the sport and, most of all, seeing me in the sport. I couldn't believe this is what they'd seen. I was subdued but trying not to pile on with negative self-talk. I had set out to do this; this dive *did not* mean that I had failed. I had two more dives to do and more important was all the work I had done, physical and mental, to get here. Still, I couldn't help but think to myself wryly, *Fake it till you make it? The water knows better! You can't lie underwater.*

My family – John, Joyce, Katie, James and Robbie in his buggy – and friends, Charlotte, Louise, Mari, my silks teacher who had become a close friend and constant supporter, and another silks pal, Arty, all met me with open arms, waving Irish flags. I wiped my face clear of any remnants of tears and ran to them.

They had watched the dive live on a phone propped up by a Coke can. The screen in the athletes' village had experienced technical problems and now was running a few dives behind. With the men's competition not starting until the next day, Nathan and his partner, along with a Danish diver called Stig, had watched it with them and explained what had happened and that

I would be fine. I was grateful for that.

When we were getting ready to leave, the screen began to show my dive, and just as I slung my gear bag over my shoulder, we heard the words: 'Claire Walsh representing Ireland, 30 metres, no fins, national record attempt.'

'Lads, we don't have to watch this – we all know how it ends!' I tried to make light of it but I didn't know if I could watch it.

My family and my friends gathered around me and together we watched my first, unsuccessful, dive of this world championship. The screen showed me making my way down, hitting the bottom and turning to start my ascent, and I don't know who started it, but someone shouted, 'Come on, Claire!'

Within seconds everyone was on their feet, cheering and shouting my name. Not just my loyal support crew, but those that had gathered in the area too. It felt like they had galvanised the spectators in a way that I feel, however biasedly, only the Irish can. My dad stood with his arm around my waist and my mum with her arm around my shoulders. Tears streamed down my face as I cried and laughed at the same time. In that moment, I was proud of myself and I was proud of them. Even when new to the sport, there are no supporters like the Irish.

If love and pride could have changed the outcome of that dive, I'd have got a white card – maybe even won the fecking thing!

My family returned home and I was able to spend some time with my friends in this beautiful town. I couldn't switch to holiday mode, but poor weather conditions stretched out the days between my dives.

After the first dive, I went for a coffee with Stig. I'd known him a few years, bumping into him at competitions I had gone to watch or in the Blue Hole, where we'd both gone to train. We got on well – he was friendly, funny and an incredible diver. Upset about my dive, I needed to figure out what had happened. He was pretty straightforward after I laid out the events of the morning.

Firstly he wanted to know why I didn't have someone with me to coach me, someone to carry my bags, help with equipment if needs be, to keep an eye on the schedule and to be there and support me in the water. He listed out a number of our mutual friends that would have been more than happy to go along with me to my dive. Again, it's a regular practice. I'd even done it for a number of people on occasions. But I felt uncomfortable asking people.

'Because I was only diving to 30 metres.' I laughed. I felt like he was describing the entourage of an elite athlete.

'Your dive is just as important to you as a 100-metre dive is to me. You deserve to have a coach with you.'

We chatted for a bit and he further impressed upon me how it's *okay* to only focus on your dive. That I didn't need to enquire after everyone, stop and say hello, check in. Essentially, before a dive, it was *okay* to put yourself first.

With that, I had a niggling feeling that went beyond identifying where I had gone wrong in my dive. Maybe it was okay to put myself first ... and not just in diving.

I spent the next days sitting with the different feelings that came up. I wrote about them in my journal. I gently deflected any thoughts that came to pile on the already tricky emotions. There was no space for *I can't do this. I've failed.* I had come so far and worked so hard just to be here. The first dive hadn't gone how I had planned it, but I wasn't injured and I still had two opportunities to dive. My ego and confidence had taken a tumble, but in actuality, this was the real test of all the skills and habits I'd formed over the last few months. I took myself to a secluded, rocky beach near where I lived and I spent time sitting cross-legged facing the ocean, breathing deeply to the lull of the water lapping the stones.

A few days later, the morning of my second dive, constant weight, I met Stig in the athletes' village. He was going to come with me and be my coach for this dive. I was nervous. I was afraid the same thing would happen despite the conservative depth I announced. But the difference was I knew I couldn't fake it till I made it.

The journey out to the boat was different. Nervous, I made sure to notice the splashes on my face, the wind whipping my already salt-curled hair, anything that would keep me rooted in the present moment. Without taking care of my dive gear and keeping an eye on my times, I found myself able to get changed and enjoy the atmosphere of anticipation.

Athletes passed by me, some on their way to their dive, some on their way back. I let them glide past my field of vision without taking my attention away from the foot I was gingerly putting inside my wetsuit leg. I started to sing. 'Regrets collect like old friends …'

'Hey, do you take requests?' someone called, knocking me out of my reverie.

I smiled. This was my go-to song and had been for years. It felt like me, not me trying to be someone I'm not. If I was singing, I was breathing. If I was breathing, I was staying relaxed. So I continued singing …

This dive was easy, unremarkable – which was exactly what I needed. I broke it down into sections, kicking at the beginning, easing the movements as buoyancy took over and I entered freefall. Touchdown, tag and turn, I made my way up, taking care to be efficient with my energy. Upon meeting the first safety diver, I thought about nothing other than what I would do when I reached the surface: *mask, signal, okay; mask, signal, okay.*

I opened the palm of my hand against the line as I broke the surface and pulled myself up out of the water.

I didn't even hear Stig's instructions but I removed my mask, signalled okay and said it.

Did I have a tag? I certainly did. I produced one from my hood and waited.

The next moment wasn't simply the explosion of joy that it might have appeared, but also one of relief, of reaffirmed trust. I had done it! I got my first white card in the World Championships and it was a national record. It wasn't a deep dive but, reminding myself of Stig's words, it was an important one to me.

'So just a few words about Claire Walsh, who has just set a new national record for Ireland. Before she was getting ready she was singing. I heard her voice, I didn't know where it came from, we didn't know where it came from. We were looking for a radio and then we were talking about mermaids and joking about an angel chorus! But she has a gracious voice and this is her way to get ready for a dive, by singing.'

The YouTube videos of my first two world championship dives are difficult for me to watch, but I never fail to smile when I hear the commentator's narration of what I do to prepare while the screen shows how utterly relieved and ecstatic I am to have successfully completed the dive.

With my CNF and CWT done, that left one more dive, free immersion. My constant weight dive had cancelled out the experience of the first and I was eager to go into my final dive … and enjoy it. Nathan had finished his competition so for my free immersion, he came out on the boat to coach me. The dive was easy, familiar and felt more like the dives we'd shared in the Blue Hole than the adrenaline-fuelled ones of the competition. It was the perfect bookend to training with him in Dahab, having him coach me and celebrate with me on my last dive of the championships.

I would talk to Boudy over the next few days and fill him in. He'd been following the competition closely online and sometimes even knew more about the other athletes' dives than I did! Our chat would take me by surprise, veering away from freediving and I would hear about his plan, his potential job that would move him to Dublin ... But I would deal with that later.

I can't say that I'm glad the first dive happened the way it did, but it certainly framed the experience as one that I would learn from for years to come. I felt like I had been presented with an opportunity to test out what I had learned.

Yeah, yeah, freediving – we've no doubt you can do that. We know it's the World Championships and that your family are here watching, not to mention all the people that have tuned in because you'd told people on social media. We know it's important to you but I'm afraid we need to see you implement the real skills: regulation, self-compassion, awareness, resilience. If this is going to benefit you beyond this expedition, we're going to have to test you in another way. Sorry!

I don't know what sort of meeting was held and where, but I did feel like it was part of the bigger picture and, perhaps, the bigger learning. To undertake this project, to plan, prepare and arrive to end up having three successful dives in the competition – well, it was too happily ever after, too neat and nicely packaged, and let's face it, real life seldom works that way. Instead I had failed, which previously might have sent me into a spiral of self-doubt and, if I allowed it, loathing but I dusted myself off, accepted myself where I was and tried again. This time with a better outcome. I had accepted help, support, and I had let people in … and it had felt wonderful. I approached my second and third dives in my own unique way, by singing – a way that was congruent with who I was and not who I wanted to be … and it had worked! I came away with two white cards and two national records. Maybe I'd try that and trust it more in the future. My world no longer felt small, at odds with the *shoulds* and the comparisons that were so easily made, and while I had often struggled to find where I fit in, I felt a bit more comfortable, more assured in forging my own path. My world felt wide open and the horizon brimming with potential and opportunities yet to come.

chapter 15

COLD WATER

In September 2019 I returned home from the World Championships so buoyed up, so full of plans and my eyes firmly set on more: more freediving, more competing, more depth and maybe even more national records. I was immersed in a family celebration, arriving home days before my beautiful littlest sister Sarah married her teenage sweetheart, Paul. My family are great at celebrations – all in, everyone putting their best foot forward – so these things seldom last just one day. This was no different. I was still in touch with Boudy. He was in the third round of interviews for a job in Dublin. He was more testing the waters, or so he said. He didn't think he would get it ... and I didn't want him to. I had no aspirations of picking things up where we'd left off, not seeing how he would fit into my life here let alone the plans I was busy hatching. We exchanged friendly texts and I put his potential move to Ireland firmly in the 'I'll cross that bridge when I come to it' box.

The morning after Sarah and Paul's wedding I saw a missed call from him on my phone.

'Everything okay? I'm at my sister's wedding.'

'Oh, I thought that was yesterday,' came the speedy reply.

'It was, but we're still here. There's drinks tonight and a family dinner tomorrow. I'll give you a shout in a few days' time.'

I told you, we don't do these things by halves and poor Boudy was baffled!

Hungover, tired and emotional, I wrapped myself in a duvet a few days later, grabbed a cuppa and dialled his number, settling in for a catch-up.

I told him about what it was like to be back, the family time, how happy Sarah and Paul had looked, the epic sing-song that still had my voice croaky, how the extraordinarily hot September weather had eased me back into life in Ireland. I also told him that I was thinking of going to Cyprus for the Infinity Games Depth competition, one of the last of the season. I felt I had worked so hard, and while the World Championships were an experience, I was capable of so much more than my performances at it. I wasn't heading off because I didn't know what to do but because instead, for once, I knew exactly what I wanted to do: I wanted to continue diving. I wanted more experience under my belt and to explore what it was like to compete in a slightly less pressurised environment than a world championship. I felt that things were beginning to slot into place and I had so much more in me. That with time and trust, more depth would open up below me.

'So that's all my news anyway. What about you?'

'I got the job. I'm moving to Dublin.'

Off I went to Cyprus.

Off he went to start the long paperwork trail required to move to Ireland.

I competed over two weeks of competition dives, learning more about the sport, feeling more potential for what I could do, and came back determined to work on my fitness over the winter and return next season ready to move to the next level of diving.

But this wasn't going to happen by haphazardly booking trips last minute. I needed a strong base to do it from, both physically and literally. I continued to work on my fitness, but sought to create some stability in terms of where I lived and the work I did. In a delightful universe-having-my-back moment, I was offered a house-sit in Crumlin. It was minimal rent that I could afford and a place to myself. I couldn't believe my luck. I started offering breathing and introduction to freediving courses. I hadn't had the nerve to do anything like that before but I kept my goal to the fore of my mind: to split my time between Ireland and working, and away and freediving.

That was my dream, and as long as I kept that clear in my head, it didn't leave much space for overthinking and self-doubt. I gave myself another project. Why? Because I wasn't going to go cold turkey; I wasn't going to finish one project and ... rest? I needed some form of structure, and I had got used to working within the perimeters of a challenge, so I decided to do 30 swims (or dips) in the sea in November. Freezing my bum off in the Irish Sea was something I've always just done – it wasn't a 'thing'. No 'wild swimming', no 'swimrise movements', I was usually in the company of men and women in their 70s who pottered down in their dressing gowns to dip like they had done every day for years. No phones, no photos, no hashtags, just their morning routine, like their cup of tea or brushing their teeth.

It felt like if freediving was one side of the coin, sea swimming was the other. Different activities but they were both linked, both a part of me, and I knew that having spent the last five months in much warmer water, if I didn't get back into the Irish Sea straight away ... well, I was hardly going to start in January.

The idea of wading into the winter waters is always greeted by the uninitiated with an exclamatory 'Are you mad?'

Maybe I was, or *maybe* this is the very thing that kept the madness at bay. Some days, life got in the way and I couldn't make it out to the coast from my new spot in Crumlin. I tried to keep those days to a minimum because they meant only one thing:

double-dip days. Have you ever tried to wriggle into cold, wet togs on a November evening? The lashings of rain pelting you in the face, cheekily reminding you that you're going to get wet anyway? No? Well, I don't recommend it.

The great thing about going down to the Forty Foot (or Sandycove during a stormy day) at any time of the day was you were never on your own. You could rely on there being another swimmer or, at worst, someone out for a walk that you could ask to hang around until after your quick dip. One evening I was coming towards the end of my 30-day challenge, quickly changing under my towel, seeing my skin prickle with goosebumps as it was exposed to the cold November air.

'How is it?' I asked the person walking in the opposite direction, eyeing the bluish-red skin and goosebumps.

'Ah, not bad. It's grand once you get in.'

Liar.

Best get this over and done with.

I walked down the steps in Sandycove and pushed off the bottom step, slowly turning in the water to take in the sight behind me. The street lamps beyond the small beach lit up a spectral mist that hung low to the ground. Feeling much later than it was, everything was still. Quiet. It was like a suspended moment in time, like winter was holding its breath, preparing for a big exhale of colder weather to come. A pause exquisite in its eeriness and full of anticipation.

I can't believe I would have missed this.

Glancing out the window and seeing mist, I would have ruled out going for a walk and venturing outside, favouring a blanket, the couch and a cup of tea instead. But my daily dip, one of the final numbers to tick off, marched me out to the car and over to Sandycove. Now I wasn't just out in it, I was a part of it – a tiny speck but still a participant. Part of the inky blackness that surrounded me and merged with the horizon to stretch overhead. Humbling. Tiny. I felt privileged. *Maybe this idea wasn't so mad after all ...*

Thirty November swims flowed without interruption into 'December swims because I like the routine' – not quite as catchy, but equally as important. I sent Boudy pictures of frost on the ground, shortly followed by the chilly-looking water in Sandycove that I'd just emerged from.

'Do you know what you're in for?' I teased him.

A flurry of cold-face and snowflake emojis followed. Just as I had melted in Egyptian summer, he would be tested by Irish winter.

We were on good terms. I'd made it clear to him that I wasn't interested in pursuing a relationship. If coming to Ireland and this job was the right move for his career, by all means, come. He could be assured that he had a friend here and that I'd do my best to help him get set up. I was transparent (or maybe blunt) about the fact that I was dating and we found a rhythm between us that was playful and friendly. I couldn't wait to show him my favourite spots near where I lived.

I loved the Forty Foot but I wanted to try somewhere new. I'd followed a photographer on Instagram, Niall Meehan, and had been mesmerised by his images captured at sunrise in the cove in Greystones. Emboldened by anonymity, I slid (or stumbled) into his DMs and asked if I could join one morning.

'Anytime,' came the almost instant, enthusiastic response.

'Sunrise, tomorrow?' I shot back before I could change my mind.

They're all so … huggy! was my first impression of the Greystones Swimrise crew. Each person I was introduced to enveloped me in a warm hug. So many people, chattering excitedly as they stripped off unselfconsciously. I threw down my gear beside Niall's, more than a little intimidated at what I feared might be a clique I was merely observing from the outside.

'C'mon!' A woman beckoned. *Yvonne, is that what she said her name was?* I checked the ground – *Yeah, purple dryrobe. The woman in the purple dryrobe was called Yvonne.*

I followed Niall in and stayed close to him in the water. *You're a big girl, you can do this. They're only people*, I reassured myself in my head. I know that I seemed confident walking up and introducing myself to a group of strangers. But what was going on inside was another matter.

Niall was easy to chat to and it felt like, despite only meeting, we'd loads to catch up on. I followed him in the water, eager to see what he saw. I didn't realise the time going by or that everyone else had got out and they were now clutching cups of tea brought down to the beach by Steve and Dave Flynn, collectively known as the Happy Pear.

I clamped my teeth shut to stop the chattering and looked for tell-tale signs of the cold in Niall. It was like he was in different water. Camera focused on the surface, he moved in and out of the light, completely in his own world and impervious to the cold.

'I might head back on in.' I want to say this sounded casual, offhand, but I'm guessing the truth would be closer to stammering and frigid.

I was glad to be on my own as I hobbled back up over the stones. Used to the smooth concrete of the Forty Foot, these stones felt like broken glass on my cold feet. I'd seen the Happy Pear on Instagram; I had followed their stories of a wholesome lifestyle and welcoming community. Welcoming or not, no one was ready to hear the swear words spill out of my mouth as I made a beeline to stand on my towel, which I threw straight on the ground.

Two women shoved the most delicious walnut cake into my mouth as my cold fingers fumbled with the zip on my dryrobe.

'Oh wow, this is delicious. Sorry, can you repeat your name for me, please?'

'Detty, like in Bernadette.'

A woman with the bluest, most sparkling eyes I'd ever seen stood beside her. They were probably in their late 60s and radiated energy and vitality. If this was what these sunrise swims did, I was ready to sign up.

Each morning was similar to the first – cold swims and warm chats followed by coffee and seedy cookies in the Happy Pear. I found myself making the trip from Crumlin, where I was living, to Greystones as often as I could. I felt ... a part of it. I would have previously considered myself more of a lone swimmer (lone but not solo) but these people opened up a new dimension to an already favoured activity. It was, without any cynicism or even a sardonic eye-roll, a community – and they opened their arms and pulled me right in.

My living situation changed, and two months back from Cyprus, I went from Crumlin to the temporary pit stop of my auntie's in Bray. By mid-December, I had sorted out somewhere for a month's time. But for now, Bray was a lovely 'beside the sea' spot to spend Christmas, with the added bonus of being a quick 15-minute drive from the cove.

Christmas Eve swims, those in-between days and New Year's Day swims were spent with this eclectic bunch of people. I knew little about what they did or their families, favouring instead the salty chats that veer off the path at delightful and unexpected turns.

I had broached my house hunt with determination, focusing on securing a base from which I could travel to start chipping away at my freediving goals. For the first year in a long time, I was building a long-term game plan. I would not travel at the last minute as a reaction to not knowing what else to do. I would plan, I would prepare and, most of all, I would embrace this slightly different way of doing things and go about it with purpose and maybe even a sense of pride, all the while being energised by this new early morning routine that I soon wondered how I had lived without.

'So he's arriving next week,' I declared before sinking my head underwater for an icy dunk.

'Are ye ... together?'

'No, no, not at all,' I spluttered, trying to shake off the brain freeze. 'He's coming over to work. I'll help him get set up and then I'm sure I'll hang out with him the odd time but no, Jesus, no! I'm not interested.'

I wasn't lying.

I couldn't see how what a 37-year-old Irish woman and a 26-year-old Egyptian boy – I mean, man – wanted could line up. I had moved past spending time with someone when I didn't see it going anywhere. I preferred to be on my own, to focus on my own plans, my own goals. If someone came along that aligned with that, super.

The lady doth protest too much, methinks.

I met my friend Mari in Sandycove for a swim and catch-up.

'So when are you getting married?' she asked, straight-faced.

I rolled my eyes and explained the situation. It was met with a 'We'll see' and a knowing look. I shook my head but I wasn't that bothered by it. I'd probably have done the same. But I had flights booked to Mexico in April and flights for Dahab in June so I wouldn't be here for a good part of 2020 … or so I thought.

The weekend Boudy arrived in Dublin I was due to move into a house-share in Rathmines. I'd been packing up my stuff from my aunt's house (it never fails to astound me how much crap I can accumulate in a short space of time). My car was loaded ready to deposit the boxes before I picked him up from the airport when an email came through.

> Tenants of Rathmines … one month's notice … selling the house.

The *fucker*! He had to have known this when I agreed to move in.

Reader, though my writing is peppered with frequent effs and blinds, I'll spare you the details of what came out of my mouth at that moment. Let's just say, I got really creative. It didn't have to be perfect, it didn't even have to make sense, the phrases just needed to cram in as many bad words as I could think of. This put a major spanner in the works. I was livid … but another part of me just shrugged. I was used to this – I had got these emails and calls a number of times over the past few years – and though I was aching for a base, a place to come home to where my things were on the shelves and in the wardrobe, I felt lighter about it than I had previously. It was an absolute pain in the arse but something would work out. I reapplied my lipstick and checked my reflection. There. You wouldn't know that merely five minutes ago I had railed like a demented, outraged sailor.

I had only pulled up when he came running out of arrivals with his one bag slung over his shoulder. 'Where's the rest?'

'That's it.'

We hugged and I glossed over the awkwardness with incessant chatter. 'How was the flight? Are you tired? Where is the hotel they're putting you up in? How was the flight –? Oh, I already asked that.'

Despite my I-know-what-I-want/I'm-not-interested protests, I found, to my surprise and horror … I was nervous.

We arrived at the city centre hotel that pumped sickly sweet scent throughout the reception and lobby, so much so that when you helped yourself to the complimentary tea and coffee you could taste it from the cups. The bedrooms were small, standard size, I suppose, for being a five-minute walk from O'Connell Bridge.

'You're welcome to stay here if you want.'

I eyed the set of twin beds. *What are you doing, Claire?* a voice cautioned. I thought of my belongings being in one place while I still lived in another.

'Sure.'

♦ ♦ ♦

February 2020 passed in a blur of packed house viewings, the same faces turning up to each one.

'Did you see that one in Stepaside?'

'No, it was already gone by the time we got an appointment.'

'What about the one in Blackrock with the guy outside shouting at the people parking their cars?'

'Oh yeah! That was a bit mad. The couple that worked in Deloitte got that one.'

'Ah great, fair play to them.'

We all crammed into en suites, admiring the space while ignoring the breath of the people behind us on our necks. Reluctant participants in the Hunger Games of Renting, it was every person for themself. May the odds ever be in your favour.

I was a woman on a mission. Finding a place to live, one where I could unpack all my things, was really important. In a little over twelve months, I'd done six moves, six rounds of moving boxes, trying to figure out what I'd need for the next few months and what to leave in the boxes scattered between my parent's attic, the theatre and the boot of my car. My books, my possessions, my keepsakes: I wanted them all together. I felt differently, more assured in myself, and I wanted to call all my belongings, all the parts of me, home and consign that nomadic way of living to a different era. I threw myself into this task, not acknowledging the other purpose it served: a distraction. I convinced myself that Boudy and I were just enjoying a *brief* continuation of the Dahab bubble, but once I found somewhere and got settled, real life would recommence. I looked for one beds, two beds and three beds. Boudy, with the email address containing his real name, Abdelrahman Talat, never got a reply to any of his enquiries.

'I don't believe you! What are you saying in it? Here, copy this and send it and I'll send it from mine. We'll see what happens.'

Sure enough, the next day I had a reply in my inbox and he had none. Every time.

We decided to pool resources, maybe get a two-bedroom place for myself and Boudy. I started to position myself in a sisterly role, while at the same time trying to find a home for both of us. Okay, okay, I can see the gaps in my logic *now*. Perhaps delusional or maybe trying to convince myself, I just needed it to be sorted and this approach seemed to widen my chances. I couldn't afford a place on my own. He was struggling to get viewings at all. Neither of us was wild about spinning the wheel and sharing with a stranger. I put my blinkers on and tried to look at the situation, however naively, from a practical standpoint. This wasn't an ideal solution, but it was a solution. Any whisperings that urged me to be cautious were shushed by my plans to compete in Mexico in April and then head to Dahab to train for the summer. I had a plan and I was sticking to it. I needed to get a place to live and get settled, Boudy would stay in Ireland working, and the situation would sort itself out.

I won't pretend I had a sense of what was to come a month later with Leo Varadkar's speech that brought home the seriousness of the situation, that maybe this wasn't 'just a flu' that was happening far away. Still, I felt a sense of urgency and threw myself into the task with mounting haste. I needed to find somewhere to live for me and my flatmate, Boudy.

♦ ♦ ♦

We moved into a three-bedroomed apartment in Bray the second week of February. Morning swims had temporarily gone by the wayside, and I felt the stress and uncertainty of the last few weeks in my body, in my thoughts, in my breath. Flicking on the indicator at the last minute, I exited the M50 early and headed towards the Forty Foot. I needed to unclench. I was sure I had a pair of togs in the car somewhere, maybe the boot or, if I was unlucky, under the seat, still scrunched up in a towel from my last swim, whenever that was …

I had missed the routine. You don't need to spend long on any social media platform these days before you come across someone extolling the virtues and benefits of cold-water swimming.

I don't like the person I was going in but I love the person I am getting out.

I missed the space, I missed the moments carved out in my day just for me, an opportunity to claw my way down out of my head into my body. Moments that acted as a diversion, a road block for racing thoughts that, if left to their own devices, would keep gathering momentum, abandoning control and, often, reason.

'Oh Jesus, this is delicious.' Maybe my tone was veering on the indecent, but God, this felt good.

My fellow swimmers didn't seem to mind. Standing a few metres away was a woman in a bikini, eyes closed, fists under her chin, clenched against the cold. 'I'm doing Freezbrury.'

Busted. I was never all that subtle in my staring.

'Oh, cool ... What's that?'

'It's a challenge started off by Damien Browne to raise money for mental health. First day of February you do one minute and then build each day. Today's the eighth so I've to do eight minutes.'

'Fair play! Best of luck with it.'

Interesting. I think I'd seen on Instagram that Niall was doing something like that. I wondered how I'd fare. I thought I might wander down to the cove in the morning and join him. Start my time in Bray as I meant to go on.

'I'm going down to the cove in the morning for a swim, do you want to come?' I shouted in later on to Boudy, who had long since finished unpacking his *one* bag while I was still clambering over my mountain of boxes to get to my bed.

'No! That's crazy!'

'Come down with me anyway. You don't have to get in.'

The next morning I introduced my flatmate to my cove friends. He couldn't be coaxed into the water. I bobbed up and down in the biting grey water and looked back at Boudy on the beach, now cloaked in someone else's dryrobe. Yvonne had taken pity on this poor unacclimatised Egyptian, shivering on the shore, looking on in disbelief. My Freezbrury minutes up, I hopped over the broken-glass-stones and threw more layers on him before starting the task of dressing myself with shaking hands.

Later I heard from Nathan. 'What is it that you're doing?' He had seen my antics on Instagram and questioned their relevance.

It wasn't *directly* related to freediving – okay, it had nothing to do with freediving at all – but it provided a shortcut to something I associated with freediving: mental strength and stamina. The first few weeks of the new year had not derailed me, but undercut my certainty, my assuredness in my plans for what I wanted and how I would go about doing it. This was a way – okay, an extreme way – of checking back in with myself, of stripping externals away and listening carefully to the dialogue and signals between my mind and my body.

'It's called Freezbrury. Day one is one minute and you build from that until the 28th – actually this year's a leap year, so the 29th.'

'Right ... why?'

Good question. I suppose the simplest answer was 'To see if I can'. I felt compelled to test my resilience, like dipping the stick into the oil in your car – you're just checking.

It's not like I feel I have to prove myself to others, but I do feel the need to prove myself to myself. I like all-in projects. Maybe moderation is a skill I'd be better served developing.

So I made a rule, I'd stay in the water as long as I could stay comfortable. Not until I was cold, but when I let go of relaxation and started chattering uncontrollably, it was time to get out. It was a challenge I would allow myself to do if I framed it as a challenge of exploration, not punishment.

That required a certain mental approach, paying attention to my breathing, positive affirmations, being curious about the sensations beyond the discomfort – not unlike freediving.

Every morning, Niall and I would wade in, starting our timers. There was an unofficial rota of people that joined us. Ken often took the first slot, his calm demeanour and fascinating stories distracting us and starting us off on the right foot. Others would join with songs and general divilment. They'd leave after a few minutes, dashing off to make their trains to work or to drop kids to school. It would be just me and Niall for the middle part. We checked in: how did we feel today? Tired? Feeling it a little bit more? His camera helped pass the time, as I once again was on the lookout. I didn't want to miss what he could see.

Someone would invariably join us for the last part, usually Jay. She entered the water with energy and mischief that had us looking forward to her arrival every morning.

'How long is left?'

'Too soon to check,' we'd both say in unison.

Nonsensical stories and guffaws of laughter helped us count down the last few minutes.

'One minute left,' Niall would declare.

'Jesus, that went quick today,' Jay would exclaim in disbelief.

'Jay, if I could feel my arms, I'd dunk you underwater!'

Waiting for us on the beach were people ready to help us get dressed, thrusting cups of tea into our hands and instructing us to 'Open' as dense cookies were shoved into our gobs.

It truly was a group effort.

We hit our walls on different days. Day 25 stands out in my head. It was a cold, wet, miserable day. Not many people made it down to the beach, so it was just me, Niall and 25 minutes to endure. We still had to do this tomorrow, and the next day, and the next. I was teetering on the boundary between 'exploration' and 'punishment'. I was tempted to abort. Deflated and dejected, we waddled woodenly up the beach, dressing in silence and forgoing the customary post-swim coffee.

I needed to have a chat with myself if I was going to show up tomorrow.

The whole challenge had consumed far more of my time and energy than the minutes in the water. If I was going to finish it, I would have to reframe my thoughts. No more *I can't believe I have to do it again tomorrow* dread. The simple fact was I didn't have to. I chose to. It was difficult and certainly there was a sense of *I've come this far, I might as well see it through.* But that didn't seem like a good enough reason. I thought about freediving and my thoughts landed on a workshop I had done with a coach years before, shortly after my first competition in Dahab. After our sessions where we worked on technique and equalisation, he instructed me to swim around the Blue Hole.

'Swim around the Blue Hole?'

'That's right, off you go.'

I swam around the perimeter of the Blue Hole, tweaking my kicking technique, trying to take on board the feedback he'd given me. I put my focus on my body, trying to streamline my position in the water, the efficiency of my movement ... I arrived back at the buoy.

'What did you see?'

I hadn't seen anything. I was so busy working on the different elements that I hadn't taken in any of my surroundings.

'You are in one of the most beautiful places in the world. You don't have to do this – you *get* to do this. If you're not taking moments to enjoy this, your surroundings, this sport, what's the point?'

I was 25 days into Freezbrury; what was the point? It was time to apply some of the mental strategies I used in freediving, my favourite being 'playful curiosity'. I had robbed the phrase from Jim Henson's biography, describing his approach to bringing inanimate objects to life and creating the lovable bunch of characters we would later know as the Muppets. For my brain, it was like flicking a switch and feeling not only a sense of relief but a spark of excitement. Not driving towards a specific goal, I'd play the *What if* game.

What if I sang a song while in the water? Did that distract me or did I find it hard to concentrate?

What if I focused on my breath when I felt really cold? Were there any relaxation techniques that I could use here?

What if when my mind is starting to send thoughts out to sabotage my attempts, I say, *Can you wait a minute, please?*

Strategies, games that nurtured mental strength and mixed it with a sense of playfulness that brought a smile to my lips, that unfurrowed my brow and helped me see that I don't have to do this, I *get* to do this. A curiosity that also brought with it the knowledge that on the other side of discomfort is a wealth of joy and sense of autonomy that far outlasts any 29-minute stint.

The last four days were the easiest ones we did.

Day 29 fell on a crisp sunny morning. With a carnival atmosphere, easily a hundred people gathered on the beach at 7 a.m. to join us for our final Freezbrury swim. Music played out of speakers, bunting marked a finish line, and blankets were spread and covered with cakes and cookies and flasks of coffee to fuel the warming-up process. Freezeberries from around Dublin had come to join us for the final hurrah. Caught up in the merriment and craic, we lost track of time in this watery playground that hovered casually around 6 degrees, exiting the water minutes after the half-an-hour mark. Beautiful ceramic medals displaying waves were made by and hung around our necks by Yvonne as we huddled for photos and warmth. It was some of the best craic I'd had in years ... and it was only nine in the morning. We'd still swim tomorrow and the next day and all the way through March, but we didn't know that this big celebration would be the last of its kind for the foreseeable future.

For the next few weeks, towel rolled up under my arm and togs dangling precariously from my coat pocket, I would shuffle down to the seafront, crunching over sand that had frosted overnight.

I had settled into this new way of living, this lockdown, as much as any of us could. It didn't feel real but it stretched out far beyond the two weeks of restrictions that we'd initially thought.

Foreign countries and freediving trips felt pretty far away, but so did my family in neighbouring counties. In those days of fear and 2- and 5-kilometre radiuses, my friends in the cove were a world away, though only around the corner of the Bray coastline.

The sea on my doorstep was my reprieve. As plane tickets to warm waters were refunded and held as vouchers, my morning swims took on a new meaning, a new importance. Not only were they a semblance of routine in days that bled into one another, they were also now my daily adventure, my dangling carrot and, often, my favourite part of the day.

Our apartment had seen work and events be cancelled, held many worried chats about money, comforted us as pangs of loneliness, fear and uncertainty ricocheted off the walls. It also saw many backgammon games and hosted binge-watching marathons of box sets that made us snort tea out of our noses with laughter.

Most importantly, it heard shy questions whispered tentatively. 'Okay, if we were to go out, be in a relationship, how would we get around –?'

Those conversations were as routine as my swims, my brain firing questions, creating hypothetical situations to make sure I wasn't going into this blindly, no matter what the circumstances.

In those months, we shared our dreams, what we wanted for the future, and Boudy's calm certainty both baffled and intrigued me. We could make it work. It wasn't going to be easy. There was a big age gap and even bigger cultural differences.

But Boudy believed we could.

He was kind, emotionally intelligent in a way that I had seldom come across in men my age; he supported my dreams and, for some strange reason, he *got me.* He could intuit meltdowns or moments of self-destruction before they happened. Scrambling to create work out of thin air, like many, I had to pivot to try and earn money. I had worked so hard to build momentum that I railed against the deadly combination of rising frustration and too much time on my hands, against feelings of uncertainty and helplessness.

So instead, I fought him. I resisted us.

'You're too young, too different, too ...' Anything I could lay my hands on, I'm not proud to say, I flung at him.

I was worried about what people would think, what my family would think.

I argue that I'm an extroverted introvert. If that's the case, Boudy is an introverted introvert. We have very different ways of interacting with people, with cultural aspects coming into play. I place value on the ability to chat, to both involve and include myself as well as other people. It's not a skill that's come naturally but one that I've had to learn – am still learning. On the other hand, Boudy was, is, quiet. Locked into an eternal battle, what level of engagement did or didn't qualify as being appropriate and what bordered on being rude was often the *Aha!* moment. Or more specifically, an *Aha!* argument. 'See, I told you it couldn't work.'

Much of it was hypothetical – it was just us – but small interactions left me questioning how we'd function in public once the world opened up again. It was a lot to think about, to anticipate, but as the months went on, it was something, we realised, that we would figure out with time.

For now, I relied on daily swims, joining the pilgrimage of dryrobers penguin-waddling down to the seafront. Early in the morning, the beach was dotted with people locked in their own little worlds, wading into the water.

The pre-dawn skies, the craning my neck to hunt for gaps in the cloud. Will we get a light show this morning? The bite of the water, the gasp as a rogue wave hit my shoulders before I was ready. The string of curses that exploded from my mouth. It was part of my routine: creative expletives, a wrinkled nose and face pulled into a grimace … and then I'd breathe. Closing my eyes, focusing on slowing my breath, calming down my mind and releasing my muscles that had tensed against the cold: these breaths were my daily nod to freedive training. They were a little reminder of all the time spent focusing on my breathing to prepare to hold it. Integrating it into the swims was a comfort, a reminder and a little whisper of *I haven't forgotten you.*

chapter 16

SOFTER

'I think I'm going to make a run for it.'

'Good. I think you need to.'

'I'm nervous! Will I book my flights?'

'Do it, before you change your mind or before we go into another lockdown. Go!'

I opened my laptop as Boudy went to our bedroom to get my credit card. I smiled listening to the sound of his bare feet padding down the hall – no matter the weather, he was always barefoot at home. He laughed at the notion of slippers and only put on socks when he had to, when flip flops weren't an option and he *had to* wear shoes. If left to his own devices, hail, rain or shine, he would be barefoot or in flip-flops. You can take the boy out of Egypt …

He was no longer my flatmate but my boyfriend.

Seven months of Covid, of being largely confined to our apartment together, had given us the space to figure out how we might move forward. It gave me the time I needed to begin to trust and to get my head around the idea. At some point during the summer I had met up with my aunty Louise for a walk and a coffee, and she had asked me about the guy she'd seen in the background of the Zoom quizzes.

'Oh, that's my flat–'

The word stuck in my mouth. Calling him my flatmate, even as a pretence, felt wrong, unfair to him and disrespectful to time we'd spent together. But I had to tell my mum first ...

I drove out to Leixlip the next day. I was surprised that she was surprised. Mum, like most mothers, has the uncanny knack of just knowing things. She had fears and concerns; I didn't mind that – sure, I had similar ones that had taken over a year, since meeting him, to dispel.

What if he decided to move back to Egypt? How would the cultural difference impact our relationship? I assured her I'd thought a lot about this, and at the end of the day, he made me happy. From that moment on, she and Dad welcomed Boudy into the family with an openness that, still to this day, makes me so proud of my folks.

It had been an intense seven months but a simpler way of living. I no longer dared to make plans: freediving, work or other. Everyone tried to scramble to adapt to living, working and socialising from home. Like everyone else, with no possibility of in-person work for the foreseeable future, I had to move online. I ran Zoom singing classes and breathing workshops. I did corporate talks on breath and wellness.

Mental health was suddenly as commonly mentioned as the daily case numbers, the restrictions and uncertainty introducing a new demographic to the obstacle course of thoughts and feelings that I'd run for years. There were days that I found difficult – the ennui, the strange feeling of isolation, the precariousness of the whole situation – but I managed. Strangely, I took comfort in the fact that any thoughts or feelings had come from the wider external environment, not from a place deep within me. If I was anxious, it was understandable – many people were. It wasn't indicative of a fault-line in my make-up that was crackling below the surface. I didn't thrive in this limbo-lockdown but I managed. We managed.

By October 2020, I spotted a gap, an opportunity to go diving. Egypt was open to tourists, and according to my friends over there, Dahab carried on largely without restrictions. I hesitated but Boudy nudged me to go, to salvage some training in this hugely eventful but at the same time completely uneventful year. Boudy stayed at home, our home, and I travelled to Egypt to freedive, to do what I love because I love it. I had no expectations – I just wanted to dive. I wouldn't be lured by the competitions that were coming up. Yes, I wanted to compete and, yes, there was much I needed to work on, but I was there (I genuinely couldn't believe it) and I just wanted to dive for me.

It was difficult to adjust. Life there had carried on as normal. No masks, no restrictions, hugs and handshakes all over the shop. It was a lot to take in and it showed how much we had, *I* had, got used to this other way of limited living.

I was going to work with Nathan for a few weeks, and on my first day we headed to the Blue Hole. We had all the depth we needed access to in the bay in front of the Lighthouse area but for my first day, my first opportunity to dive in almost a year, it had to be in the Blue Hole.

I wasn't nervous, I wasn't excited, I was ready. I had slept well. I had put myself through a rigorous routine before I started my session. I was ready, I was present. That was all I needed. Ali welcomed me back. I drank my ginger and lemon tea, as was customary, and I took in all the changes that had taken place over the last 12 months.

Aqua Marina was now in a different location, a short walk to the Blue Hole rather than just in front of the entrance. Ali had already put in place measures to minimise any minor inconvenience we potentially could experience from being in the new location. His staff carried our buoys and equipment down on a cart and would bring back our flip-flops if we wanted to leave them on for the walk down. As always, he was anticipating problems and wasting no time in averting them before they had a chance to arise.

'Hello, old friend,' I whispered when I finally slipped my head underwater (I was notoriously slow at getting ready). Nathan had already set up the line and was floating in the water by the time I'd made it over.

'The line is set to 20 metres. So let's take this nice and easy. Take all the time you need to breathe up. Enjoy your dive.'

With five-plus dives a session, three to four sessions a week per however many weeks, months and years I've spent training, it's mad how some dives stand out; some dives you can remember like a slow montage of feelings and sensations.

This dive was easy, surprisingly so. Easy and, more importantly, relaxed … my body remembered. As if something that had lain dormant was stirring, unfurling and ready to awaken. Like when I return to my parents' house having not been there for a while, and I open the door and am met with that distinctive Ryevale smell. I can't believe I'd forgotten what that smelled like. It's comforting and reassuring and it smells like home.

The Blue Hole, my body and freediving were welcoming me home.

It was different travelling and having someone waiting for me back home. Not that Dahab had ever been a place where I'd dated much. Well … except for Boudy. I tended to park romance, or anything else, when I was there. It was a small community with everyone knowing everyone else's business. But having a boyfriend, a partner, at home made it different. It lent a certain reassurance that I hadn't had before. It was difficult, too – we went from living in each other's pockets for eight months to spending two months thousands of miles apart. I both missed him and welcomed this space to myself, knowing he supported me.

And it was space, space to soak up sun and warm weather. Space for endless afternoons of coffees and chats, cards and backgammon, broken up by dips in the mid-20s water and ended by the sky changing colour. Some people had been here all throughout Covid, some had just arrived from Europe, all had different opinions on the year that had passed and what was yet to come. During the day, I basked in this freer way of living. In the evening I scrolled on my phone and saw the numbers in Ireland, rising cases and whispers of a return to lockdown. I felt a complete jarring of worlds.

I was back diving, an activity that nourished my soul like no other, but I also thought about Boudy alone in our apartment, and everyone stretched to the limit with fatigue and frustration about being confined to their tiny bubble. My heart was in two places and, without realising, fear and anxiety crept in.

This time here was too precious, too much of a gift to squander getting locked into an anxious cycle.

If I was going to stay in that, I may as well go home. I went back to all the practices around freediving – stretching, breathhold training, meditating, journaling – and looked at the techniques I could use to ground myself, protect my energy, ease up on that tight sense of 'heldness' and need to control.

♦ ♦ ♦

'You're different this time.'

'In what way?'

'I can't put my finger on it.'

I'd just surfaced from a dive and Nathan was looking at me sideways.

I shrugged. A lot had changed since the summer before the World Championships. Was that only a year ago? I still sometimes had to pinch myself that I was here. All the plans, the travelling, the training, the competitions that had evaporated over 2020, none of that mattered. I was here and I got to dive. That excitement could still make me splash the water in a burst of giddiness, my legs, treading below the surface, giving an extra flutter for flare.

'Okay, okay, calm down. You still have to do your dive.' But he was smiling. He set the line to 45 metres. I had decided to focus on bi-fins this trip. It was new and, despite my poor legs not having had much exercise the last while and struggling with stamina, I was enjoying it.

'Take your time. The line is ready for you.'

I closed my eyes and couldn't help the smile playing on my lips. I was already really happy with how this dive went.

Holding onto the buoy, I kept breathing, my legs burning from lactic acid (and lack of base training). Thoughts rushed into my head. *I can't believe how far I've come. I can't believe I remember how to do this!*

I was so grateful to myself for taking the leap and, once again, putting myself in this environment, for coming back to this sport that seemed to shine a light into all the dark corners and bring clarity to my mental muddy waters.

But I could reflect on all that later. I parked those thoughts and urged myself to stay in my body with the sensations, to savour this feeling: the exquisite combination of the thrill, the comfort and the accomplishment.

'I'm okay!' I sang.

'Yes, you are.' He laughed. 'That's it. You're softer.'

Softer. My mind immediately jumped to the weight I had piled on, the muscle I had built relaxing, giving me a softer outline.

C'mon, Claire, you know that's not what he meant.

Softer.

I thought of the opposite of needing control. I thought about that *heldness* that keeps your body captive when chasing that state, locked and rigid with tension.

The word 'softer' told a different story. It fudged the harsh expectations I might have imposed on my diving and brought to the fore the sheer delight I felt just to be able to do so. Softer spoke of an acceptance, a warmth, a place from which there were many possibilities because your gaze could take in all the opportunities in front of you.

'Softer? I'll take that.'

♦ ♦ ♦

Getting photos taken by Janna scared the shit out of me. Janna is a photographer based in Dahab, and she had taken pictures of me the previous year when I'd spent the summer there. Towards the end of my trip I'd contacted her about a session. It was both empowering and terrifying in equal measure, but it had forced me to look at myself in a different light. I could do with investing some energy in that. Plus she was really talented and the photos were beautiful, perfect for filling up the little squares on Instagram when I was back in Ireland sitting in my tracksuit with Sudocrem on my face. In a fit of 'seize the moment'/'sure, look, why not', I contacted her once I had returned to set up a similar session: the 2.0 version.

'How would you describe water?'

Oh that's easy, I think to myself. 'Dynamic. Powerful. Calm. Feminine.'

'Yes. Good. You will use these words when in front of the camera. They will make you comfortable.'

I blush a little. The words came easily when asked

to describe the water, but I think maybe I'd also leaked how I would like to describe *myself*.

Worst of all, she instructed me to be … sexy. Now, I don't think it's just me, but that sort of instruction either has me looking like a rabbit caught in headlights or searching for someone to make eye contact with so I can nod my head towards her in a 'would ya listen to yer one!' sort of way.

Since I'd arrived in Dahab, and often when I was dropped into an environment filled with youthful, lithe bodies in barely there bikinis, I felt frumpy. Old, unable to ground myself and feel secure in my beautifully soft and freckled body. So what did I do in those situations? I played up to it, of course! I acted boyishly (whatever that means in this day and age) and I threw remarks before anyone else could. I made sure I planted my feet firmly in the 'one of the guys' camp, creating distance between myself and those girls because, in my head, there was a gulf between us.

Even removing the element of flirting and scanning male company for eligible (albeit temporary) companions, it still unsettled me. In my late thirties, I wanted to move towards loving my body how it looks, knowing what it's been through and what it can do, and detangle my sense of confidence from how I look. Fairly straightforward, eh?

Having my picture taken (at all!), but in this case with Janna, rattled all those insecurities. It shook them up so vigorously that I couldn't help but believe that when they settled again I'd be a little bit closer to my goal.

'Ooooh, sexy,' she exclaimed, looking at her monitor. 'Mr Claire will love this one.'

Jesus Christ, I thought. *What has she captured?*

She handed me the camera to take a look. *Woah!* I barely recognised myself. Scrolling through the shots, I was shocked at what she had been able to capture. They were clearly me, but a different side of me, a side that maybe I denied or layered over with humour, deprecation and doubt. In those photos I saw myself. How would I describe them?

Powerful. Calm. Dynamic. Feminine.

They were the images I was going to hold up to myself when I went home. This woman, I *knew* this woman! I knew all her internal battles but I also saw so clearly what she's capable of. I'd bring her home with me, and the two of us would conspire, dream up a plan. A plan to return to Dahab in a few months' time, to train, to freedive. A plan to move my work, my career, in a direction that I'd never have dared pursue. And the biggest realisation was that I wanted that plan to include Boudy. *Habibi.* The time apart had given me space to look at our relationship, to see what he was to me and to know he was part of my future.

I love it when a plan comes together!

chapter 17

BURNT POPCORN

After coming home from Dahab I was determined to improve my fitness levels. After 10 months of Covid restrictions with pools and gyms closed, like many, I had segued into a more sedentary lifestyle. I never really got into online fitness classes. I'd be lying on the floor doing my plank holds and spot a patch of dust underneath the couch. *I must have missed it while doing the hoovering. Come to think of it, when was the last time we'd hoovered?*

I'd slink out of the frame – don't get me wrong, not to hoover – and click on the kettle. *Meh, not today. I don't feel like it.* I'd give it a minute or so before feigning an excuse or claiming internet-connection issues. Coffee and scroll was more my tempo. Smacking my lips together, figuring out what I'd like to accompany my cup of coffee. A bit of lemon drizzle cake would be lovely – I could whip up a batch and it'd be ready in an hour. Much better use of time! That's how the 2020 lockdowns were spent: skipping exercise and baking to meet my every sweet-toothed whim.

Visiting Dahab, getting away for what felt like a lucky-escape trip, helped me lose weight and remind myself how much I valued the ability to move in my body, a sense of, not quite endurance, but being able to turn my hand to different activities – hiking, a silks class, snorkelling – and not have it be my exercise for the day. It was just something I *did* and enjoyed. Dahab was something of a reset and I came home mid-December hoping to keep up what I had started.

So 1 January, 2021, our bellies full of turkey and selection boxes, Boudy and I decided we'd do the cliff walk to Greystones and back. Not exactly a challenging hike but a decent length constitutional that would blow out the cobwebs. It was one of those perfect Irish winter days. Cold, crisp and sunny. We wrapped up and I threw my togs into my bag. It was the first day of the new year, and I had big plans for it. There was no way I could mark it without a swim.

We walked. We took pictures – some of the two of us together, me trying to look photogenic and him trying to see out from heavy eyebrows that tend to fall into 'resting frown face'. We never get the shot.

We argued – I can't remember about what. Possibly I got cranky when he was going too fast or patronising me by being too slow. Maybe he got grumpy with me for wanting to have the chats or talking too much ... All in all, a fairly standard Claire and Boudy couple's walk.

We walked back along the seafront, deciding where to eat. We were both veering towards becoming hangry and couldn't make a decision. We finally agreed that I'd go for a (reluctant) dip and Boudy would pick up food from Dockyard 8. Deal.

I stripped off my layers and stood with my togs in my hand, pausing a fraction too long in the why-the-fuck-do-I-do-this stage. No, it's the first day of the year, a new year that will hopefully be a better one. Start as I mean to continue: in the water.

Bray beach was packed with the once-a-year swimmers braving the water for the first and only time for 2021. They had picked the wrong day to do it. It was fucking freezing. A group of regulars, who were heading off on a *swim* swim, took out their thermometers and dangled them in the sea: 4.8 degrees. Now *that* was cold.

I couldn't get comfortable in the water. I regulated my breathing, focusing on elongating my exhale to help get over the initial shock of getting into the water. I let my toes float up to the surface and adopted a serene look on my face. That usually worked. Calm on the outside; focus on relaxing the muscles tensed against the cold water. The inside usually follows. I observed the New Year's Day dippers thrash and squeal in the cold water. I was a regular and used to this. There was no way I would allow myself to even hint at my discomfort. Why *was* I so cold? Okay, I know it probably had something to do with the sub 5-degree temperatures, but I had been in yesterday and the day before. I ran through my checklist: period due? Nope. Hungover? Nope, I had been tucked up in bed by 9.30 the night before. Particularly tired? Nope, please see aforementioned 9.30 bedtime. Fuck it, just one of those days, I guess. Listen to your body etc. ... time to get out.

I pulled my clothes on over my not-quite-dry-yet skin. Boudy returned with no food in tow. 'Closed,' he said. Biting my tongue against the 'did I not say to google it' retort, I nodded. Fer feck's sake, I was starving.

As we walked off the beach, I saw a text come through in An Chlann, the family WhatsApp group.

'James and I have symptoms of Covid and are going to get tested.'

Fuck – 1 January. I last saw them on 25 December.

Yes, we'd had 10 months of Covid and restrictions and Zoom quizzes and online challenges and definitely there was angst and frustrations at being hastily shoved back into our 5-kilometre bubbles on 26 December (meaningful Christmas, my arse!). It was safe to say we had lockdown fatigue. But the numbers were relatively abstract. Everyone knew someone who knew someone who'd had it. But the virus itself still felt at a distance. I'd just travelled through three airports and spent two months in a country without restrictions. I wasn't necessarily afraid of it. My attitude was if I get it, I get it, as long as I don't pass it onto anyone. That was my fear.

'They'll be fine,' Boudy reassured me and we spent the rest of the day watching old episodes of the *Great British Bake Off*. Aside from occasional exclamations of 'temper the chocolate first, you gobshite', it was a quiet day, typical of this restless but lazy, stuck-inside Christmas season.

The next day I woke up feeling tired and a little bit achy. Funny, now that's a fairly standard feeling, and I have to remind myself that it wasn't the norm then. We had done 30,000 steps the day before – that was probably it. I pulled my duvet onto the couch. *Do I want to go for a walk today? Do I fuck!* I sent Boudy around to the shops to get provisions. I was not budging.

We had the obligatory squabble over which movie to watch. I begrudgingly extended my couch–duvet fort as Boudy put on a bag of microwave popcorn. I was settling back onto the cushions with a mug of ginger and lemon tea in my hand when behind me Boudy said, 'Shit, shit, shit!'

'What's wrong?' I asked.

'I burnt the popcorn.'

I looked at him, confused, as he pulled the smouldering bag out of the microwave. Now, I am *very* pernickety about smells. I've been known to faint in the perfume section of the Duty Free. Scented candles, barring a few exceptions, make me feel queasy and the smell of cooking on my clothes or hair really, really bothers me. Growing up, I would wear a lab coat and hat to protect my hair and clothes from any smells of cooking. Burnt popcorn is in the top three of offending smells, along with burnt toast and the smell of a cooked fry (greasy-spoon cafés are my worst nightmare).

Boudy fired the bag out onto the balcony like a live grenade and looked quizzically at me. Normally by now I'd be flinging windows open and cursing to the high heavens.

I couldn't smell anything.

I ran around to the cooker and put my face *right into* the batch of ginger and lemon tea we had brewing. Nothing.

Shite.

And that's when I knew I had Covid.

Covid itself wasn't the worst. I mean, it was definitely not 'just a flu'. I was achy, my skin was sore, I had a sore throat and a headache, and I watched *GBBO* from a crack in the blanket swaddling my face because my eyes were sensitive to light. I was groggy during the day and restless at night. But there was an air of inevitability. It seemingly was everywhere. Though everyone had been pretty strict in the lead-up, limiting contacts, and I'd tested and PCRed after returning from Egypt, someone had had it when we all met on Christmas Day.

We counted our days. Boudy started to feel sick and we split up the apartment to not infect or reinfect one another. On day four something changed for me. I didn't necessarily feel worse but my breathing changed. It was quicker and ...well, not right. I had been out of breath going from my bed to the bathroom. But now I felt out of breath lying down.

I rang the doctor and he told me to go straight to A&E. Woah there! Hold your horses – it's not that bad. Hospital seemed like a wild overreaction. I was just a little bit breathless. Or was I? I couldn't be sure. I was a mild case of Covid, just a step above asymptomatic. No need for all this. But it niggled at me all day.

I think a big part of it was that because I spend so much time paying attention to how I'm breathing, I knew something wasn't right. No matter how I tried, I couldn't slow it down. I rang the doctor again and he asked me to count the number of breaths per minute. The answer had him repeating his 'go to hospital' instruction. It really didn't feel that urgent, but at the same time I didn't feel right.

'If it persists or gets worse, call an ambulance. Go to the hospital.'

I was a little rattled and went to the kitchen to get something to eat. The walk took it out of me. We live in an apartment – granted, it's a big one, but it's hardly an epic journey from my bedroom to the kitchen. I didn't know what to do. I was afraid of it getting worse during the night and scaring Boudy. As I sat there, food uneaten, I began to get a pain, a weighted feeling in my chest. Okay, time to go.

We called an ambulance and the paramedics were at our house in no time. It was surreal enough to have other people in our apartment let alone two tall men in hazmat suits. They did some short checks and decided they wanted to bring me out to the ambulance. I was still able to talk and could joke with them but they wanted to be sure. I grabbed my dryrobe to throw over my (no bra underneath) hoodie and tracksuit bottoms, and runners to go over my stripey knee-high slipper socks. I think if ever there was an outfit that represented my experience to date during the pandemic, that would be it!

Boudy helped me down the stairs. It was all grand. They didn't think things were too bad – they just wanted to be sure. This was precautionary. Yet, it was a strange feeling to be a relatively young and fit person, who not weeks before was holding their breath for minutes at a time, 50 metres under the water, withstanding 6 atmospheres in pressure, now standing at the top of the three flights of stairs, wondering, *How the hell am I going to do this?* I felt like I had put on someone else's shoes by accident and these ones were too small. They didn't fit. And neither did my lungs. It felt like I was in someone else's body.

At the ambulance I reluctantly said goodbye to

Boudy. Thank God this wasn't serious. But as I saw him through the window, unsure and hovering on the path outside, my mind flashed to stories and news reports about families unable to visit their loved ones. Of nurses sitting with patients as they battled on their own. Both Katie and Sarah had had babies during Covid, a new niece and nephew, Joy and Ollie, added to the brood. It was so different to when Robbie had been born. There were no hospital visits, and my heart constricted at the thoughts of my brothers-in-law waiting in the car park for their one hour of visiting time.

Dan the Paramedic Man was efficient as well as kind. He ran tests and kept me entertained. My go-to in any medical situation is to have the craic, be as friendly as I can and show them that I'm not *that sick*. I waited, taking a sneaky selfie to send to Boudy, smiling to reassure him and showing the hack of me to make him laugh. And then suddenly, I was pooped. The adrenaline and the effort of wanting to be the most craic/most compliant patient had worn off. I couldn't talk. Around then they decided to bring me to the hospital.

I was torn between not telling any of my family and knowing that I'd have to let someone know but I didn't want to scare them. I settled for Matt. I knew he wouldn't panic. I was going in; it was more than likely fine. The evening had already taken a turn I didn't expect, so just in case.

Arriving at hospital in an ambulance was nothing short of surreal. I'd, thankfully, never been in one before. It was so strange that my instinct was to document it, to record it, to – what? Put it on Instagram? No. Watch later? Hardly. As they wheeled me in, I caught myself and left the phone in my pocket.

The hospital looked very different to any visits I'd had before. It was uncannily quiet but humming with the suggestion of chaos happening elsewhere. The numbers that dictated and determined the levels of restriction the rest of the country had were all here, in the hospitals. It was the epicentre of the pandemic, that which restrictions and lockdown were based on. This is where the doctors and nurses, the frontline staff, were putting in hour after hour as I sat at home and binge watched all six seasons of *Schitt's Creek*. I was a little bit in awe and a bit mortified that I was in here taking up a bed and their time.

I was put in a room and given a Covid test. Then some blood tests, then an ECG and a chest X-ray were done. I waited for results and dozed. All came back clear – including the Covid test. Hang on, what? Dazed, I peeled off the electrode patches from the ECG. What the fuck was going on? Had I imagined it all? What was wrong with me? The paramedics who had brought me in and the nurses had disappeared, needed elsewhere.

Was I free to go? How the fuck was I going to get home? I waited in the cubicle, unsure of what to do.

'Are you still here?' A masked face popped round the door. 'You were discharged.'

'Oh, sorry, I thought I had to wait for –'

But they were gone, their runners squeaking on the tiled corridor.

Helen came to pick me up. Unsure of whether I did or didn't have Covid, I sat in the back with the windows open, both of us wearing masks. I arrived back to the bottom of the three flights of stairs early the next morning, looking up. I *didn't* have Covid? The stairs shouldn't be any problem then.

I climbed the three flights in three-step intervals: 1, 2, 3 rest. 1, 2, 3 rest. 1, 2 (little pause) 3, rest ...

I reached our front door and let myself in. Shuffling down to the bedroom, I let my dryrobe fall to the floor and I fell straight into bed. I think I only ever let myself be scared in retrospect.

Once Boudy put his arms around me (*home* home), then I could have a cry. What had just happened? What the fuck was wrong with me?

He has this magical way of soothing me that completely validates my feelings, makes me feel understood and comforts all at the same time. There really is no feeling in the world like it. Mixed with the delicious smelling, cosy sleep fog around him, I fell asleep to him whispering that everything was okay, we'd talk about it all in the morning.

We carried out the rest of our isolation period in the apartment. Boudy's sister, a doctor in Saudi Arabia, informed us that false negatives weren't uncommon. I was displaying many of the symptoms as well as being a close contact of several people. She said to take it that I did have Covid. I don't know why that mattered, but it did. Invisible illnesses: are you imagining it? Are you exaggerating it? The symptoms feel very real and you know you wouldn't wish it on your worst enemy. Still, a lot of energy is put into explaining that you really *are* sick. It's probably fair to say I have a bit of a sensitivity to illnesses that are … not tangible? My old doctor would often say, 'If you had a broken leg you'd have to get it treated and rest and rehab – depression is no different.'

It is different. I can see a broken leg. More importantly, other people would see the cast and say, 'Oh shite, Claire, you broke your leg! Maybe put those bags down. Don't be trying to carry them up the stairs. In fact, you sit down – I'll bring them up.' Labels aren't important and certainly in this day and age there's an emphasis on fluidity. God knows I've rejected diagnoses before … I didn't particularly want to have Covid but as I had all the symptoms – I wanted the name. I wanted proof it was real.

As always, Januaries are never fun, and by the time you get to what feels like January 75th you're ready to shake off the month, move forward and make some progress into the year. This was even more true by the end of January 2021. I first had symptoms on 2 January and had finished my period of isolation by 12

January. My symptoms were mild to moderate, and I can't deny that I got quite a fright with my trip to hospital. But as I finished my 10th day (as were the regulations at the time) I looked forward to getting back to normal – whatever normal was in those days. Our plan to return to Egypt at the end of January would be pushed back to March. I'd get over Covid. I'd recover, regain fitness and it'd be a small blip contained to the first month of the year.

No one likes January anyway.

chapter 18

SAME SAME, BUT DIFFERENT

It all feels strangely familiar, like déjà vu. I've been here before, felt like this, but of course I haven't.

My fingers hurt. A strange ache around my knuckles, like my hands are at the early stages of atrophying. It's muscular, or rather in my joints, but at the same time I can feel it in my teeth.

My knees are the same, as are my feet. It's not exactly painful but more so really uncomfortable.

I've overdone it. Hands, knees and feet aching mean I've already done too much. Cracks of light that are reaching me underneath the blanket hurt my eyes and travel straight to my stomach, making me feel queasy. I'm already on the couch, blanket over my head, but I don't know if I've caught it in time.

'Can I get you anything, love?'

I give a faint smile. I love his use of 'love'. He says it so fluently, so tenderly, that it injects new meaning into this overused Irishism. Maybe he feels the same about how I now use *habibi*? I don't know exactly where he's picked it up but it's gas (another one of his favourite expressions but I know the origin of this one: my mum) and so genuine at the same time. It makes me feel ... warm.

I shake my head slightly and reach out for his hand. Words are scrambling in front of my eyes and my mouth feels slack. He gets it. I don't need to talk or communicate right now. I know he'll let me be. I need to rest. I need to recharge. I don't know if that'll take two days or two weeks ... or longer. I feel helpless, vulnerable. Mostly scared. Once again, I feel scared.

I don't know when I knew I had it – it took a while anyway. Covid came and went and I clapped myself on the back for, once in my life, taking things slowly. But by February, enough was enough. Time to get fit, up my steps, use the rower, get back to swimming and other various 'new year, new me' proclamations. Still in lockdown, I decided to go for the lowest hanging fruit: increasing my movement. Ten thousand steps a day, that's what they say, isn't it? My work was based on the computer, gyms and pools and pretty much everything was still closed, so I decided my best bet was to head out on a walk as early in the day as possible. I couldn't rely on pottering around the apartment to hit my target. It had to be a *walk* walk, arms swinging with intention. Anything that I did beyond that was a bonus.

Off I went. I tracked a few routes around Bray that would have me at my target in or around the hour. I listened to podcasts. I lapped the gate in front of my building just so I could return home on all the zeros. And, boy, was I smug when I punched the code into the gate. *Gosh, it really makes a difference to your mood, doesn't it?* I thought to myself, conveniently forgetting how much I hate going for walks and the complaining I'd done 70 minutes earlier. There was an extra spring in my step as I opened the door to the apartment block. *God, I feel good – it's really amazing what you can achieve when you get up and start your day off the right way. Why haven't I done this –? Shit. The stairs.* I had forgotten about the stairs. We lived on the third floor and we had no lift. *No bother to me*, I thought breezily and skipped up the steps.

Three steps from the bottom I was leaning on the railing. My heart was pounding and my lungs felt like they were about to implode. Legs burning and heavy like lead, I set off at a slower pace. Break it down, a few steps at a time. Slowly, slowly. Three steps later I needed a rest. My walker's high already evaporated, I was in disbelief at how this felt. I could feel my eyes start to fill and the back of my throat constrict as my frustration mounted. I got a wave of that I'm-in-the-wrong-body feeling I had the night the paramedics came. Not only was I in the wrong body but these lungs didn't fit at all! Three flights of stairs is hardly an endurance event, but standing on the sixth step, I didn't know how I would make it up. I could call Boudy, but I was embarrassed. Besides, he couldn't exactly carry me. So I had to approach it the same way I would any other physical challenge: piece by piece. If I broke it down into bitesize tasks, I wouldn't get overwhelmed. Just focus on the task in front of me, the actions required and I'd get through.

I concentrated on my breathing. Breathing in through my nose, making sure my belly pushed against the waistband of my leggings, expanding on the inhale. I climbed step one, step two, step three and I stretched out my exhale. Rest. Deep breaths. Off I go.

Opening the door to the apartment, flushed, sweating and out of breath, I flung my earphones on the table. 'Nice walk?' Boudy asked. I probably was aiming for something offhand but I'd left that somewhere around step number ten. I turned my back so he couldn't see the tears fall. What was wrong with me? I didn't leave the apartment for the rest of the day. I was not doing that again.

When I set off to conquer the 10K mountain on day 2, I paid attention to how I felt going down the stairs from my apartment. It felt okay – maybe I just needed to get used to it. It's not like I hadn't gone up and down the stairs during January. Yes, that was painfully slow but I'd had Covid then. This was February and I was better now. Most of all, I had *decided* I was better and that I was going to get fit again. I was drawing a line under the experience. Surely that counted for something. Denial masked as determination, as a carousel wheel of 'you can do it', 'no pain, no gain', 'push through' platitudes spun in my head.

I returned from my loop a little bit more tentatively this time. Walking on flat ground was fine. Yeah, my legs felt a little tired from yesterday but that was to be expected. I thought back to two months ago. I had been in Dahab, diving. Walking from place to place. I came home and started back running. Over Christmas we had lapped the park beside our house delighted with ourselves! We were continuing the promises we'd made while I was away: to work on our fitness, to eat healthier. No more impromptu lemon-drizzle-cake baking for breakfast. How was that only five weeks ago? The stairs felt every bit as difficult today. And the next day.

The following day, I didn't go out.

I repeated that pattern for most of February. Exercise, exercise, rest. Exercise, exercise, rest. Then it switched to exercise, rest, rest. Rest, rest, rest. Repeat cycle.

I'm used to having days on the couch. I've always recharged this way. For years, I'd interspersed gym sessions and hikes and silks classes and swims in between rest days but every week or so I'd have a day on the couch and switch off. It was more to decompress. I'd put on a series and let it roll from one episode into the other. Tinder or Bumble would keep me company. Over endless cups of tea and a veritable feast of junk food, I'd chat to Barry or Darragh or Colm or Dave while what felt like season 96 of *Orange Is the New Black* played out on the screen.

The dating apps element may have disappeared but the habit of crash-couch days was long ingrained, and during lockdown it had enjoyed a triumphant comeback. But this felt different.

On these rest days, the sitting room with the blinds pulled wasn't dark enough, screens hurt my eyes, and our once gloriously comfortable couch hurt my back. I felt overstimulated simply by having my eyes open. Soon my bedroom was the only place dark enough, my bed the only comfortable place. *This feels a little too familiar*, a sing-song voice would caution. *Is it long Covid or is it actually …?*

No! I wanted to shut that idea right down, there and then. This wasn't depression. I didn't feel like I had felt before. I knew that feeling shit or frustrated or lost was a reasonable response to my situation. They were normal emotions to feel and proportionate to what was happening. Still … I didn't trust them. The hard part was that physically I felt incapable of doing that one-step-at-a-time shuffle to begin to move beyond them.

'It's fine,' I'd repeat to myself. 'I'm just tired. I just need to rest more.'

Resting means at some point you feel replenished. I could never quite catch up.

As a child, every once in a while a stomach bug

would go through the house. I'd wake up and the first port of call was to inform Mum I wasn't feeling well. (Apparently I had a broad sense of what classified as not feeling 'well'. I have not yet lived down the fact that as a not-so-young preteen I woke my mum up to tell her that I had a blocked nose.) Mum would fetch the sick bowl (I presume every house had one?) and I'd spend the next 12 hours retching my guts up until there was nothing left but bile. Tummy sore and tender, I'd sip flat 7-Up (the reason I can't stomach the stuff to this day) on the couch under a duvet.

The first sign of recovery was beginning to feel hungry, but there was still a long way to go before I'd be allowed to have anything to eat. Eventually I could have some toast. If I kept that down and hadn't vomited in nearly 24 hours, I'd feel almost back to normal, aside from my tongue feeling fuzzy from the taste of 7-Up. I might even want to go out to play. Then I'd have my shower. A brief rinse, I'm not even talking about a hair wash, and I'd feel like a deflated, discarded balloon. Drained and a little shook, I'd melt back onto the couch. Maybe I'd wait till tomorrow to go out to play.

For years after, the metric of 'getting better' after any illness was to see how I felt after a shower. February pushed through to March and I constantly found myself shook and like that used-up balloon, well past its glory days. Ten-thousand-step walks fell by the wayside and soon tasks like walking to the bathroom, preparing food or drying my hair left me feeling weak. No matter how many times I tried to create a rhythm, a momentum, I kept finding myself back at square one. I wasn't moving forward: I was falling backwards.

If I could just push through. Maybe this exhaustion was temporary, like returning to exercise after a long spell out of the routine, when you'd wonder how you'd ever undertaken a walk or run or gym session so effortlessly. There was an inevitable adaptation period – maybe this was it? I wasn't fully convinced but I had to try.

Aware of this cycle, this lethargy in another context, I couldn't *not* draw comparisons. I knew I had to do things that would help me feel better, that would give me energy. Maybe not tomorrow but definitely sometime next week. I had the right idea – I just didn't realise that, in this case, those efforts, activities, needed to be something very different. I'd start with a walk and trust that it'd pay off. One foot in front of the other and gradually put in little tasks, little accomplishments that would accumulate into something beginning to resemble progress.

So I'd walk and then the next day I'd walk again, maybe move a little bit around my apartment. Feeling brave, I'd wash *and* dry my hair. There, didn't that feel better? On a roll, I'd pull out a knife and the chopping board and start to prepare a soup, a curry, something laden with veg to boost my struggling immune system. 'This will be great to have ready when I get back from my walk tomorrow,' I'd sing to myself, delighted with the semblance of routine and momentum.

I never did get out on that walk the next day. I was flat on my back on my bed in the dark, unable to shower or sip the flat 7-Up, if I'd been so inclined.

'Long Covid' they call it. I don't know who first mentioned it. I'd heard of it but it was still very abstract. Smugly or naively or a combination of both, I presumed it was 'out there' happening to *other* people. I knew of no one who was experiencing it.

'But sure we're all tired,' was the response that came when I tried to explain how I felt.

'No, it's not a normal tired. I feel like I just can't operate, can't replenish my energy no matter how much I nap.'

'Nap? I'd love to be able to nap during the day. Wait until you have children ...'

I'd stop talking in a mixture of shame, guilt and frustration. Of course I didn't know the tiredness of being a new mother, or a mother to young kids or pre-teens or teenagers during a pandemic. And honestly, I don't know how I'd have managed it. Listening to how friends and relatives juggled the roles of mammies and entertainers and educators and cleaners and working women and so on, all within the confines of their house and the 2-kilometre restrictions, cut off from their support systems ... I thought they were heroes.

But another part of me wanted to scream, 'I'm sorry you're tired. I know you have children and I'm sorry I don't. As much as I'd like to "just get on with it"' – *I. Just. Physically. Can't.*'

It wasn't like I was draped across a chaise longue, having a glass of wine placed in my hand and grapes dangled enticingly above my mouth should I feel peckish. I was sitting on the floor of the shower, Boudy washing my hair because I just couldn't quite manage it.

The title of 'who's the most tired' is much-coveted, but the thing was, I didn't *want* to compete for it. This feeling, these symptoms, reduced somewhat clumsily to the word 'tired' was the best I could do to describe this cycle I found myself stuck in and the list of day-to-day things that I was able to do that was shortening by the week.

Pace yourself.

I was trying to operate within 'spoon theory', an idea of quantifying energy as spoons and how simple, everyday tasks can leave a person with very little else to work from. It has been used by people with chronic illness and a friend, Niamh, had introduced me to the concept. It was a useful metric. She had become an incredible resource (and friend), particularly relating to all things spoonie.

'How's the energy today? What's the spoon count like?' she'd regularly text.

'Meh, not great,' I'd reply. 'Never mind the spoons, I fecked the whole cutlery drawer out the window.'

Even now I laugh. I laugh at my sheer inability to have a corporeal understanding of the idea, of the phrase, 'pacing'. It went against all my natural instincts and inclinations. Always that hare over tortoise, I am an all-or-nothing sort of person. Going slow still means I'm probably thinking about one thing while doing another and making a mental note to google something for later. If I'm *actually* going slow, I've stopped.

Pacing was mentioned to me in early March and I probably nodded politely but failed to understand its relevance to me and how I was feeling. Well-intentioned but I didn't think it applied to my situation. That was for people with illnesses, chronic illnesses. I understood why it was necessary but it just didn't fit with how I liked to do things. Thanks, but no thanks.

How delightfully cute/naive/arrogant I was to think I would have any say in this, to think I was impervious to having to take these measures because of all I used to do. That because doing things was something I'd built my identity on, because doing things was what I'd relied on to cope or muddle through when things got difficult, I might somehow be immune. That they didn't apply to me. Doing things and at the pace I wanted was so important to me, to who and *why* I was, it's understandable why I gripped so tightly onto the idea, the ideal of returning to the me before. It made sense. I had worked really hard, through more error than trial, to build up more positive ways of approaching things. I couldn't contemplate having to start all over again but instinctively I knew what had worked before wasn't going to carry me through now. It was an inconvenient instinct, one that I tried to ignore, but each time, each setback, pointed me in the direction of the reluctant realisation that I was going to have to learn a new way, a gentler way. This was an entirely new game with a new set of rules. But to think I could simply opt out? Come on, Claire …

It wasn't rock bottom but it was uncertain. It brought dark days, and huddled together at night, Boudy and I worried about my health and what the future might look like. But I am not averse to gritting my teeth and navigating an unbeaten path. I knew I'd have to re-evaluate my plan, my strategy. Resting and proceeding gently, managing energy and respecting boundaries, my boundaries. And most of all saying no – saying no and not spilling out words of justification, explanation and apology. Saying no and *not* beating myself up for it afterwards. It's funny, seeing it written down, listed out. Resting, managing my energy, creating boundaries: it's obvious that these were never my strong suit. They were always my weakness, a set of skills that let me down, that I never invested time or energy into developing. Now I was being forced to. Sure, I recognised the opportunity to learn and add some new tools to my bag of tricks, but knowing and acknowledging didn't stop me internally throwing a tantrum, like a sulky teen flinging her bag onto the table to reluctantly start her homework.

I would do it, but I also knew from experience it would take time and before I reached the other side, whatever that might look like, it was going to be difficult and there were going to be pitfalls ... plenty of them.

chapter 19

TANGLED NECKLACES

I pulled into SuperValu, turned the car off and took out my phone for a quick scroll before heading in to grab lunch. *I fancy soup*, I thought as I opened Instagram.

There she was, another female freediver, blitzing Irish national records. I no longer held any of them. It wasn't that big a deal. We're a small country and we're only beginning to be represented in freediving competitions. Our national records are very achievable and small compared to world records. Women were bound to come along and try their hand, push the records deeper and deeper and help grow the sport in this little country of ours. That is what I had wanted … right?

I shook my head in an effort to clear it and smiled, pleased for her. I knew the athlete. I had wished her luck on her dives and waited eagerly to hear how she'd got on. I'd congratulated her success and meant it all. Still, a hollow feeling settled in my stomach. *Good for her.* I rallied as I grabbed the bags for life out of the back seat.

'Claire Walsh, free immersion, 50 metres, national record attempt.'

You'll have already left the surface for your dive when the judge calls this after you. It's exciting, the NR beside your name, and irrespective of depth, it adds a little something extra to the feelings before a dive.

Would I ever hear that again?

Never mind national records or competing, I wasn't sure if I'd dive again. Even the prospect of travelling *anywhere* to train, let alone compete, felt so far beyond my capabilities.

I was struggling to get to grips with Long Covid Claire and I was even more unsure of her long-Covid body. It does things to your sense of who you are, your sense of identity, as ways of living, doing and being feel very much like past tense. It's a funny thing not to trust your body any more. I'd ventured metres below the surface on one breath, I'd handled half an hour in 6-degree water, and I'd done so by listening to and trusting my body. Now, my lungs didn't feel like my own, my body sometimes buckled under the effort of day-to-day tasks, and my energy drained, leaving behind pains and aches in my muscles. Freediving dreams were far away, but so was the active life I'd led before Covid.

I'd seen small improvements. I'd been working with a personal trainer, Colin McEndoo. Niamh had introduced me to him because he had experience in dealing with clients who had chronic fatigue. Compounding my good fortune, my freediving sponsor, Timewise Systems, had agreed to cover the costs of the sessions. I'd kept in contact with Ronan and he had an idea of what I had been going through.

'It's an investment. You'll get back on your feet.'

Not only was the financial aspect incredibly helpful, but the simple statement of belief meant just as much.

Training with Colin was one of the fragile pieces of string that was holding together my sense of equilibrium. It was as much for my mental health as it was for my physical. Our sessions would often pause as I couldn't lift weights *and* finish my story. I negotiated exercises and, I'd guess, was a client he rolled his eyes at when he saw me coming in the door. But our sessions were a mix of ugly lifting faces and guffaws of laughter. It felt like starting all over again but he coaxed me to view it as an opportunity to build a stronger foundation – it might just take a while.

This tested every bit of patience I did and didn't have! But for all the times I managed the slowly, slowly approach, there were twice as many times when waves of frustration and desperation crashed against me. The simplest of exercises could land me flat on my back. I didn't trust my body to do anything – how was I ever going to build myself up to a point of basic fitness where I could take myself underwater?

Shake it out, Claire, I thought as I strode with purpose into the shops. *That is someone else's journey and you know that there is room for you both. Celebrate hers and get back to yours.* I was starving, time for lunch.

I can't tell you how long I stood in front of the fresh bread in SuperValu. It could have been seconds; it could have been half an hour. The sound around me was blurring and I felt like someone had grabbed the my head and was dragging me backwards through a vacuum by the ponytail. I was there but I wasn't. The people around me no longer seemed to matter and the tears splashed down onto my top.

I need to get home. I need Boudy.

Clicking his number on my phone, I willed him to pick up.

'I need you to come and get me,' I sobbed down the phone as soon as I heard the familiar 'Hello, hello!'

'What? What's happened? Are you okay?'

His confusion was understandable. I'd dropped him off only five minutes previously.

'I need you to come and get me.'

'I don't understand – you have the car. Did something happen?'

I couldn't explain it. I just knew I needed him and I needed to get home and, frozen in front of fecking Cuisine de France baguettes, I wasn't sure I could figure out how.

'Claire, I need you to breathe. Leave the shop and go outside. Slow your breathing down. I'll run around and get you.'

As soon as I was outside, the pings of blurriness that had framed my vision started to dissipate. We lived 90 seconds from the shop. I could drive home. Boudy was waiting for me outside on the path.

He didn't ask me what was wrong. He took the keys and my phone out of my hand and guided me upstairs. I didn't appreciate it fully in the moment, but it was the reassurance and grounding gesture I needed. I certainly didn't have the words to explain what was happening.

I walked straight into our bedroom and pulled the duvet around me. I howled. Boudy slipped into the room and into his normal position of the big spoon. He let me cry ... and cry and cry. Fat, snotty, soaky tears that left puddles on the pillow, that had me so congested within a few minutes that I had to sit up and blow my nose just to breathe.

What was wrong with me? Everything had been going well. I thought I had been doing the swan, swim, swim, swim below and glide on the surface. I thought I was managing. Lying on my bed I just felt so empty. I didn't feel like me and I didn't know how to get back there.

'I – wwaah–nnt – tooo – freediiive,' I howled between gulps.

'But you can go freediving,' he reassured me.

'Dunno if I'm able,' I muttered.

'Don't worry, we'll work on a plan.'

'But I don't know if I'll be able or if I'll ever compete again or anything. I don't know what I'm doing and I feel like such a failure.' The dam had been opened. I couldn't stop the floods. Failure. At what? At living? 'I don't know who I am or what I'm doing. I might never feel better, feel like me.'

My brain was flinging things at me quicker than I could scan for plausibility. Spitting out sentences, searching for possible explanations to this feeling, this shuddering stop. Jumbled explanations tumbled out over one another and I frantically searched for the clear-cut box to put this disproportionate reaction into. I wanted it out of my body, up into my head where I could intellectualise it, make sense and rationalise it. (Snort! Like that's a strong point of mine.) Instead I felt it all over my body, low in my stomach, hands shaking as I balled them into fists and pressed them against my eyes.

I had been fighting with myself so much. My body had gone rogue and was doing whatever the fuck it liked with *no* regard to my wishes or what I'd planned. A gym session? Pfft! We'll see. How about some joint pain instead? What was that? A gentle walk? Wrong again, time for a bout of fatigue that'll have you on the couch for three days, and while we're at it, I'm going to coordinate with Brain and we'll throw in some *what the fuck is happening* thoughts. How does that sound?

Like an absolute pile of pants, that's how it sounds.

I thought I was being positive, chipping away at things, working on the thoughts that came and whispered in my ear, *Not good enough. Lazy. Negative.* In that house-of-cards-come-tumbling-down moment, all I felt was a little bit lost and very tired. Mantras and affirmations felt hollow and I felt raw and exposed, for once not caring how vulnerable I was.

It was one of those days, the kind of days you feel have been a while in the making, where things come to a sputtering halt. I'd felt like this before. I'd felt like this many times, actually. It was a cyclical halt that I'd experienced at some point every couple of weeks or months and then every couple of years. It still took me by surprise each time. Every time this day arrived I exclaimed a soft 'oh'. Then I'd eaten my way through it. I'd drank my way through it. I'd dated, I'd Netflixed and I'd travelled my way around it. I knew how to dull it down, I knew how to dampen it, and most of all I knew how to distract, distract, distract.

I'm not going back there.

I'm quite good at detangling necklaces. It's not something I'd put on a CV but, nonetheless, it's a skill that I'm happy to possess. Unlike the Claire in so many other situations, I have patience with it. Slow and measured, I roll the knot in my hand, assessing which strand of the chain to gently tug that will begin to unravel a seemingly solid tangle.

When I feel overwhelmed and like that knotted

necklace, not knowing where to start unravelling, each thought pulling the knot tighter and tighter, Boudy somehow instinctively knows where to start. He gently asks the questions that I hadn't even considered.

What has that got to do with –? Oh!

As I cobble together an answer I realise its relevance. Strange. It almost takes me by surprise, like I'd been looking, searching the horizon, and then something came up behind and tapped me on the shoulder. I had been looking in completely the wrong direction.

'Is this really about freediving?'

'I dunno.' I'm not quite ready to concede. But if it's not about freediving, what *is* it about?

Maybe not freediving, but something that I associate with freediving: an alignment, a sense of cooperation between my mind and my body, an autonomy and acceptance. Peace.

With the gentle weight of Boudy's arm around my waist and the coolness of his hand stroking my clammy forehead, the fogginess and busyness of my head cleared. The *should*s and external stress that I'd been using as a distraction fell away. Suddenly so clear, I realised it had just been a smoke screen, and that something had been percolating and simmering behind it, begging for attention for longer than I'd even realised. With that there was relief, but also tears. Lots of them.

In the days leading up to this there had been moments of pure discomfort, irritation even in my own skin, metaphorically and physically. It itched. It irritated. It felt like there were ants underneath it and I just wanted to scrape it off, remove the top layer. Then I'd have some relief.

I'm not going back there.

It would have been easy to pull a duvet over my shaky body and say, *I'll decompress for a few hours here.*

But I didn't. I replayed and spiralled and flagellated. As my laptop powered to life, my tabs reopened and Netflix sprang to life, offering me visual chewing gum, soothing, seductive distractions like Salome dancing with her seven veils.

No, this day had to be different. I'd hit this point before. Maybe that made it easier to see that I had to implement changes now, not tomorrow. I knew this crossroads, I recognised the scenery, I'd noticed the signposts, giving them a quick glance over my shoulder as I scurried by.

That day something unfurled inside me, raging with a hulk-like force in a refusal to go back to those ways. I might have been pulled back to them but I was suddenly kicking and screaming. That day you would not find a nice, compliant Claire. Pissed off and eyes glinting wildly, I swivelled to face Fear.

What? What is it that you want? I'm here. I'm listening. I'm not going anywhere. No subtle hints, no prods, no pokes. Show me some fucking respect and tell me straight.

My hands were shaking, my legs felt like jelly, but my jaw was set. I would not look away first.

All we have to fear is Fear itself and in that moment, for that moment, I was done.

I could usually postpone these moments. I could trawl Instagram and 'motivational quote' myself out of it ... sometimes. But right then, I was all out of positive spin. I was the worst of the worst in social media terms. I was the opposite of 'positive vibes only'. I was sitting in The Shit and refusing to couch it in gratitude or positivity.

Change your energy.

Ground yourself in nature.

Negativity only attracts negativity.

Be grateful.

Listen to your body.

Set boundaries.

Practise self-care.

Be positive ...

FUCK RIGHT OFF!

Go be fucked.

Take a flying fuck at a rolling donut.

Make like a tree and fuck off.

Why don't you go and play a game of hide and go fuck yourself?

Take your pick.

Yeah, that story of the two wolves fighting inside us. Which is the one that wins? The one we feed. Well my 'bad' wolf was out, snarling and patrolling the perimeter, ready to go for the throat of anyone that approached offering any 'pick yourself up and dust yourself off' wankery. But instead of loading up a shotgun and aiming it at that she-wolf, I needed to let her out. She was dominant right then for a reason. She needed to roam.

She needed to howl.

So, ladies and gentleman, welcome to The Shit. Take a seat, we're going to be staying a while.

Make yourselves comfortable and remember there's one rule: no positive spin allowed.

In that moment, in The Shit, I was lifting my chin and giving the day a significance.

I had had enough.

I was not going back there.

With experience under my belt, I knew this didn't mean it was job done – in fact, it was only the beginning.

Boudy held all this space for me. It was nothing short of remarkable. In my desolate uncertainty that flipped to a raging wildness, he remained calm in the face of the storm. He listened, he redirected questions, he validated my feelings and, for some reason that I will be eternally grateful for, he understood. He sometimes intuits and understands me better than I do. The man hasn't a romantic bone in his body and still hasn't grasped the concept of why one might want to celebrate a birthday or an anniversary – a source of many gritted-teeth conversations. Then something like this happened and I was in awe of how he knew what to say, the manner in which he said it, so that I could actually hear it and not rebuff it and reroute to the worst-case scenario.

He pulled my hands away from my eyes, holding them, and told me how hard I was on myself, how determined I was and how, if I put my mind to it, there was nothing I couldn't go for. He told me of the beauty he sees in me, as I squirmed and resisted the urge to push the words away. He told me of his belief in me. How a shit day, or even days, weren't a failure, but just that, a shit day. They were only a small part of the picture. It was like hearing a really comforting story with much-loved characters until the jolt of realisation hit that he was talking about me. *Her determination, her resolve.* That character was me. His calm and matter-of-fact way had me almost believing him ...

Sitting in that rented house in Wicklow at the end of 2018 had been a starting point. The beginning of a series of decisions to put myself forward, to not just flee that moment but to think about and invest in my future. To represent Ireland in the Freediving World Championships and stand over and be proud of that decision, a decision and process that would ultimately change my life and open up opportunities that I had never before thought possible. Don't misunderstand me: I didn't win medals or discover a superhuman talent. My dives in the World Championships weren't anything special. But that doesn't mean they weren't important. Those dives helped join the dots between November 2018 and September 2019 and led me to step into the arena in a way that I had never done before. But it didn't stop there. After putting myself out there, there wasn't a happily ever after … and thankfully! Life continued on and I was presented with the same cycle but a different incarnation of challenges and I had to, once again, choose to move myself forward.

When I hear people's stories, hear their turning points, they always sounds more majestic than I imagine they were in reality. In films, we see the protagonist making a decision, possibly looking wistfully at the horizon before adopting a steely look of determination. What follows is a montage of their journey, their hard work, the struggles and the inevitable stumbles … but they always get up and keep going, all the while accompanied by motivational music that has suckers like me tearing up and willing them on.

But we can't speed through that journey. In real life, there's no fast forwarding or skipping over, there's no montage. You can't put a timelapse lens on the months and months it takes to make small changes to create progress.

And by progress I mean that swing of the pendulum, sometimes forwards but sometimes backwards. Not the up-and-up-and-up graph with little dips between. More like a ball of yarn after a cat's been playing with it: tangled, messy and with the edges frayed.

There's no hiding from the fear and self-doubt that will inevitably come knocking to question you, challenge you, throw obstacles at you to see how quickly you can adapt and test your resolve. But unlike other points in your life, you remember that moment when it felt, not brave, but like you didn't have a choice.

I am not going back there.

'There' might change. 'There' has been a crumb-covered couch in a rented cottage. 'There' has also been curled up in the foetal position in the bed I share with Boudy more than two years later. 'There' isn't a place and 'there' can happen again and again. 'There' is a feeling: it is the realisation that enough is enough. That nothing feels worse than this standstill. Nothing feels as scary as staying, being stuck ... 'there'.

That's your motivation. Not motivation itself and not fear either. It's the realisation that staying in this place, stagnant, is so much worse than any of the elements associated with moving forward that scare the shit out of you.

And, unlike that movie, you will probably have to make that decision again and again. Elements and details may vary but every so often you will hit that crossroads, make those choices that move you, however slowly, forward. I used to feel terrified by this prospect.

Now, I feel somewhat comforted by it. Just like a current that keeps pushing against me, keeping me from the shore, there are also waves that will lift and carry me in. It's about timing and trust and it feels like part of a bigger picture, a more universal cycle.

Each time I've hit that point, once I've let go of Fear and all its companions, I can see this cycle for what it is, a tide to move me nearer to what I'm supposed to be, one that won't end until I take my last breath. It is what life is made up of, the deliciously rich and at times painfully challenging sequence of crises and opportunities, growth and expansion, fear, abundance, sorrow, gratefulness and peace. It is life and it's a full spectrum of emotions and experiences.

How I approach it is entirely up to me.

chapter 20

I'M OKAY

The last few months of 2021 passed like a cha-cha-cha: a slow step forward followed by a succession of quicker steps back and in the same spot.

Long Covid. Who knew? The doctors certainly didn't. I had spent summer and autumn back and forth to my GP, being examined, having bloods taken, getting B12 injections. Everything was inconclusive and nothing helped. My doctor abandoned his already meagre bedside manner to suggest psychological evaluation because as far as he could see there was nothing wrong with me. I'm replaying the memory and relishing scripting assertive words to advocate for my care, my physical health and my mental well-being. But that's after the fact. In that moment, I sat in my chair, head down, knowing that the 30-minute round trip to the surgery would put me in bed for the rest of the day. Helpless, my words of explanation, my pleading, became choked and thwarted by my tears of desperation.

'Any history of mental illness?'

Oh fuck. He wasn't my long-time doctor but was it not in his notes, my file on the screen in front of him? Was I going to have to say it and see the look of 'Ah, that explains it' in his eyes?

I just wanted to go home. I just wanted to *be* home. This wasn't the first time I had had a doctor dismiss symptoms, dismiss how I was feeling. I had dissociated in those meetings, not seeing a way out between not being believed and my complete lack of trust.

Maybe it was all in my –

NO! I've come too far to fall back into that box. NO! That version of me is younger, vulnerable. I've grown so much, worked so hard since then. I am able to do this.

Folded in his patient chair, I took a deep breath and attempted to straighten myself. 'Yes, yes, I do have a long history of mental illness. As far as I know, details of my diagnoses and treatments are in my records. I know they were sent to the clinic. Over the years, I've been an inpatient at St Patrick's hospital and an outpatient at Cluain Mhuire. I haven't been on any medication for nearly 10 years now, and I manage any difficulties I still experience with talk therapy and the plethora of tools I've learned from my counsellor. I work hard to maintain my mental health. I appreciate you wouldn't know this about me, but I am not fabricating these symptoms, which are completely diminishing my quality of life, ability to work and perform day-to-day tasks. This is impacting my mental health but my mental health is not the root cause.

'I am intimately familiar with all the permutations of my mental health. This is not it.'

Eyes wide above his mask, he looked at me. 'I'll put you down for a referral anyway.'

That evening Boudy pulled the duvet off me and, in a rare act of ignoring my protests, pulled me by the legs out of bed.

'You can get back into bed the minute we come home and rest all day tomorrow. I know you feel shit, but we're getting a win today. You're getting in the water. Now, where are your togs?'

He usually followed my lead when it came to what I was able to do. He often threw out suggestions, offered alternatives or sometimes gently cautioned, but he never put his foot down. If I wasn't so pissed off, it might have even been a bit sexy ... but who had the energy for that.

I pulled out my dryrobe and slipped my feet into my flip-flops, which were waiting for me at the door. The cold water shocked my tired body out of its rage. I slowly turned around, taking in the shore, the shops that stood beyond it, the cross at the top of Bray Head and, finally, the horizon that spoke of deeper waters.

'I want to try a breathhold.'

'Really? In this water with no wetsuit?' Boudy asked incredulously. Static breathhold was normally done in the pool and with a full wetsuit on.

'Yup.'

'That's my girl!'

My body fought the cold and the unfamiliar sensations, but it remembered, I remembered.

'One minute thirty,' Boudy called overhead.

The lower part of my ribs started to flare with contractions, I softened my stomach, and I thought about that doctor. One part fuck you (*Yeah, that's right! You hold your breath, Claire, that'll show him!*) and another part a reminder: I wasn't weak. This wasn't gritting my teeth and pushing through; this was softening everything and letting go. This was reminding myself of what I knew, of resilience, of the ebb and flow of challenges I'd faced and overcome. This was a reminder that I didn't need to let someone else's opinion, albeit a medical professional's, dictate the reality that took the legs from under me most days. I wanted a win; I wanted a little check in with my body – it felt like we just hadn't been on the same page.

Face in the water, limbs gently bobbing with the ripples of waves, the absence of noise cleared the way for me to *hear*.

What do you need? I asked my body, promising that this time I'd listen to the answer.

I pulled my head out of the water once I heard

Boudy announce three minutes. In 10-degree water in the Irish Sea with no wetsuit and just my swimming togs on, never mind long Covid and being mentally shattered, that was an achievement! I stood up, eyes red from the salt water but glittering with that old look of determination. So much uncertainty but I knew I could still rely on myself. I knew that if I listened carefully and trusted myself, like everything that had gone before, I'd find my way through this.

Standing up, I smiled.

I was okay.

♦ ♦ ♦

Turning to face the horizon, I let my toes float up and break the surface of the water. 'Heal me,' I whispered as the water rushed over my shoulders. I watched my friends get out, hopping over the cold grey stones of the cove. I needed a few more minutes to cook.

With a soft exhale, my eyes came to rest on the line where the sky met the sea. My thoughts flickered to the sights, the potential below the surface, to freediving. *Maybe soon.* I sent out the wish, comforted by the shift from *maybe never again* to *maybe soon*. Progress in the last few months had been slow, but there had been progress. I felt stronger, not just physically but mentally. Stronger but softer, the *slowly, slowly, this moment, and then this moment* teaching me more about acceptance than I had ever learned out of the water.

But I didn't need to think any of that then. There, my body knew what to do. There, my body knew how to move. There felt like home and, despite having long since lost the feeling in my toes, I relished the sense of relief and familiarity.

'Are you having coffee or not?' someone shouted from the shore. 'Feck off and let me have my moment,' I replied, sinking my mouth below the surface to hide my smile as I swam back to the beach.

It's been a while – just a few more minutes.

I don't know which I love more, the water or the folks that I share it with. It feels like both meet me and accept me exactly as I am. Not how I should be, not as I would like to be: the Claire of that moment is fine just as she is.

'Would you look at the colour of you!'

I shrugged as I emerged from the sea in all my bluish-red, goosebumped-skin glory. I wouldn't have it any other way.

chapter 21

WELCOME HOME

'Good morning! Welcome home.'

I had always loved the drive from Sharm el Sheikh to Dahab, ever since my first time travelling it back in October 2017.

After the security checkpoint, passport number and police looking in the car to see me (I still find that part disconcerting. Do you smile? Do you try to look less threatening? Do you pretend to understand the rapid-fire Arabic between the men?) I usually try to settle down to sleep ... But I can't. The sky! The sky is a deep velvety purple, holding a fat, luxurious full moon. The mountains are lit up as if by a spotlight and look so perfectly 'Arabian' that they seem unreal, almost too perfect.

Returning year after year, the taxi from Sharm is always an exhale, the final leg of the journey – an exhale despite some gasp-inducing driving. One driver is known for using this time to update his Instagram, do Insta Lives, FaceTime. I'm pretty sure I've even seen him playing backgammon online with one hand with the other firmly placed on the steering wheel and a flip-flopped foot on the accelerator. Road safety is just that *little* bit different here.

Each time the taxi driver says 'welcome home' as we drive into Dahab while the sun comes up, I take a mental picture of these moments. Driving under the Dahab sign (click), the first street I recognise (click), catching a glimpse of the sea (click), the sun rising from the horizon, dazzling my 'travelled through the night' eyes (click, click).

Weeks or months later when I am packing up my gear, I scroll back through my mental camera roll and think back to the first morning. No matter how much time has passed, it feels longer. The merging freckles on my face mark the physical difference, the shine in my eyes hinting at the shift that's happened on a different level.

Welcome home.

This time the journey felt different. I had come a long way with long Covid but I feared that the travel and transit had stretched my capabilities to their limit. The winter in Ireland had felt long and drawn out. It had tested my resolve in many ways, and by March of 2022, I was ready for light, heat and a change of scenery. But this trip was far from the impetuous, book-a-ticket-at-the-last-minute trips of the past. We had planned for this. We had made it our goal – *we*, because Boudy knew even more than I did how important it was for me to go back. Part of me wanted to beg him to come with me, scared of the idea of being there without my biggest support.

'You'll be fine,' he reassured me. 'I think you need to do this on your own.'

It had been a long time since I'd travelled with someone, and my airport routine and rituals were well established. Still, I waited in the boarding area of Dublin airport, clutching my passport in a sweaty hand, wishing he was boarding with me.

I'd taken earlier flights before but was more tired than usual. Each leg of the trip had gone smoothly, but now that I'd arrived, I felt exhausted. Mouth parched and thick with the taste of grabbed moments of sleep on flights, a headache punched my forehead from the inside and I shielded my eyes from the light that would make me feel queasy. I felt ... old. If not old, jaded.

Thankfully the driver, Walid, who had come up from Dahab to collect me, had a boot full of bottled water. The journey that I normally loved, the one I'd thought about so often over the 15 months since my last trip, I just wanted it over and done with. I urged myself to take it in but all I wanted to do was switch off. I knocked back two painkillers and didn't even wait until the checkpoint to sleep.

'Good morning, welcome home,' Walid called. *Sabah al– al– n-something*. My brain couldn't find the word. I lifted my head from my rolled-up hoodie and wiped the drool from the corner of my mouth.

Blearily looking out the window, I saw the Dahab sign overhead. I didn't know if it felt like home but it did feel familiar. So familiar, in fact, like no time had passed at all. Familiar but incredibly surreal. Rubbing my eyes I took in the streets, trying to get my bearings.

I knew that when I thought back to this morning in eight weeks' time, it would feel 'like ages ago'. I'd feel like a different person, that so much had shifted, moved slightly to the left, making way for the feelings, thoughts and ideas that tended to get repressed at home. But like someone who downloads and looks through their marathon-training or couch-to-5K plan for the first time, I could see the goal but just couldn't visualise how I was going to get through all the different stages to reach that point. All I could do was lace up my metaphorical runners and set off.

We arrived at my apartment, my home for the next two months. I carried my backpack with my laptop, a wash-bag and earphones up three flights of stairs. At the bottom, Walid had thrown my two bags, a cumulative weight of 50 kilos, over his shoulders and tucked my long fins under his arms. Uncomfortable with this dynamic, I had fussed and tried to take one of the bags from him with the awkwardness of someone who takes out their purse to split the bill when it's already been taken care of. Do I go full Irish mammy and insist? He smiled from a refreshed face that belied the time of the day and repeated, 'No problem, no problem,' as he skipped up the three flights.

I was too tired to argue.

The apartment would do nicely. I unpacked. It was 3 a.m. but I knew I wouldn't sleep so I may as well wake up to a settled apartment. I showered and finally made my way to bed. Putting in my earphones, I began a meditation – start as you mean to go on and all that.

I'm going to be so zen when I'm going home.

I felt like my body was levitating over the bed, bone tired but humming with energy. I tried to switch my brain off and hoped that my body would follow.

What the f–?

I jolted upright in the bed. It was dark and I couldn't make out where I was. Someone was outside my door, shouting, calling. I could taste the aeroplane food from hours earlier at the back of my throat. My heart was thumping in my chest. My only chance at self-defence was an emery board I'd unpacked and left on my nightstand. I was fucked.

Seconds passed and the reverberation clicked with a file in my auditory memory. The first call to prayer: Fajr. It would seem that I had mosques in each direction because the call was coming at me in surround sound. Like when kids in the 90s used to sit on the bus and try to play the same Nokia ringtone but fractions of a second off.

I settled back onto my pillow, wiping my clammy skin on a corner of the blanket. I knew in a few days I wouldn't even hear it any more. I fell back asleep, unable to shake the familiar-but-surreal feeling.

♦ ♦ ♦

I pulled off the tags with my teeth, averting my eyes from the size displayed. Today felt wobbly enough without going down an I-feel-fat rabbit hole. One emotional crisis at a time, eh?

My brand-new T-shirt and shorts were straight out of the Irish-mammy-going-on-holidays collection: respectable, functional and comfortable. No time for anything like fashion in these hotter climates. I slipped my pale feet into my (new) Havaianas. Glancing at myself in the mirror did nothing to relieve the old-and-jaded feeling of yesterday.

Soon. Soon my face would have a smattering of new freckles and my feet would have the white marks from the thongs of the flip-flop. The sense of displacement would have evaporated and I'd have settled in like I've done each time before. I just needed to be patient and a little kinder to myself. My reflection rolled its eyes, clearly not in the humour for self-compassion.

Thankfully the weather was – wait, it was cold! I mean, I wasn't scraping ice off the windshield of a car but it was windy as bejesus and I wouldn't be going far without a hoodie. This was Dahab! This was not what I'd signed up for. Light, heat and a change of scenery, remember? I had brought one hoodie with me, and normally that got rolled up and stuffed in a bag until my flight home. Not this time.

Pulling it over my head, I headed down towards the diving area of Dahab, the bay or Lighthouse. I knew I'd bump into people I knew. I was nervous. I'd thought so much about being here the last 15 months. Now I didn't know if I would fit in any more. I was so far away from adjusting to the Dahab tempo. I felt uptight, held and as out of place as my crisp new holiday wardrobe.

Dahab folk are huggers. Like the pre-Covid cove people ramped up a few notches. Maybe it's a remnant of Covid living, maybe it's my general discomfort – but hugging that many people that I didn't particularly know felt alien. I smiled at the familiar faces, slightly jealous of their ease, and hid behind humour as I squirmed internally.

'Welcome back! How does it feel?'

'Familiar but surreal.' *Jesus, Claire, all they wanted was a* great! *Light and breezy, light and breezy, keep it light and breezy!*

'Claire! How does it feel to be back?'

'Great! Familiar but at the same time a bit surreal.' *Ah, for fuck sake, you're not even trying!*

Everything felt clunky. How I moved, how I interacted. I cringed and grimaced after each meeting, caught in one giant 'I carried a watermelon?' moment after the other.

That first day, I met my Danish friend Nanna. Of the people that I knew here, she'd reached out and asked to meet for a coffee to say hello. That felt good. It was a plan. I could work with a plan. Plus, I couldn't wait to see her.

I'd met Nanna for the first time in 2020. The freediving world is small so I knew her name and I had seen her pictures. My first memory of interacting with her was when she'd arrived in Dahab in November 2020. I had finished in the water and Nathan and I were debriefing the session. 'I like your swimsuit!' she said, stopping by our table and nodding towards my green togs with cartoon orcas splashed across them. They *were* cute – also sustainable and delightfully childish. I had gone overboard and bought several pairs. 'Thanks, I have them in sharks and toucans too,' I said, pulling the neckline a smidge higher. They might be delightful but they were no match for my post-lockdown boobs,which were constantly threatening to escape.

We'd continued with the usual 'How are you?' 'How long are you here for?' 'Where did you spend lockdown?' conversation before Nanna exclaimed distractedly, 'I'm sorry, I've just arrived from Europe. I'm a bit out of it. It'll take me a few days to adjust.'

Yes! I understood that! Arriving from 2-metre social distancing, masks and elbow bumps to no restrictions whatsoever was a shock to the system. Seeing this many people in such close proximity was jarring and it had taken me a while to adjust.

During that trip we progressed from saying hello in passing to playing the occasional game of backgammon until one day she declared, 'I'd like to go with you to the water.'

Nanna is an established and talented photographer and 'go to the water' meant doing an underwater photo session. I was honoured and, at the same time, felt the gaping chasm of insecurities split my internal landscape.

I'd left behind my cartoon-orca togs and donned a more neutral black suit as requested. Nanna suited up in full freedive rigout – fins, snorkel, mask, the lot. Heading out into the water, that swell of feelings rose up. Inadequacy. I chatted to Nanna as we kicked out, distracting myself from the urge to apologise for how I looked, that I didn't look like other underwater models, and a feeble attempt at self-deprecation in an effort to appear glib about the whole situation.

I think that's how I first really got to know her, that photo session. Being in the water with someone, either on a buoy freediving or in front of their camera, you get to know them in a different way. There's an element of vulnerability that you can't escape. Conversation seems to skip the inane small talk and you meet each other on a new level.

Nanna was encouraging in a way that made me pause before the automatic deflection of a compliment slipped out of my mouth. She seemed genuinely curious, like she had caught a glimpse of something and was determined to see more. Coaxing and encouraging, her focus took over and she went to work issuing directions before sinking below the surface, face pressed against the viewfinder. I started to let go, switching off my own thoughts and going along with the experience. I trusted her. It reminded me of those times I'd had my photo taken by Janna, but this felt a little bit rawer. More like me. It was liberating, empowering and oh-so tiring. Nanna's English is perfect except for one phrase she seems to keep getting confused.

'Okay, we do it one more time,' she repeated each time she looked up from the screen. I stopped believing it after the tenth 'one more time'. Taking a deep breath, I exhaled forcefully through my nose, as I tried to sink my buoyant body below the surface.

We returned to the shore 45 minutes later – she blue-lipped and shivering, me trying to navigate the steps through my tiny salt-water-slit eyes. I would be dripping sea water from my burning nasal passages for days. We sipped ginger and lemon tea, a new bond formed. I found her open and honest curiosity about me both uncomfortable and amusing. She had decided she liked me and wanted to get to know me and that was it. So she became my remora, a fish also known as a suckerfish, whose fins act as suction so that they can attach to larger marine animals. Nanna was going to be my friend and after an afternoon in the water, laughing so loudly that it echoed around the bay and gazing down the lens of her camera, I didn't mind the idea of that one bit.

So I was excited to see her again.

Excited waves and a flurry of hugs and smiles marked our reunion. 'There's a new coffee place. We'll go there.' A new coffee place where I live in Ireland is a regular occurrence. Every couple of months a brightly coloured but dimly lit coffee house pops up, boasting different roasts and blends and a display case full of vegan, gluten-free and paleo treats. No big deal. A new coffee place in Dahab was a different thing entirely. There the places that served good coffee and smashed avocado on sourdough were few and far between. This was exciting!

We settled down with our coffees and slices of vegan carrot cake and set about catching up on what had been an eventful year. I relaxed a little into my seat. Chats, conversation, catching up with a friend. Maybe it was all going to be okay.

Wait, am I talking too much? Am I listening enough? Is she giving me a funny look? Does she think I'm an idiot? Shit, maybe I don't fit in here. Wait, no, she's smiling. That's it – I'm doing it! I'm doing interacting!

Social muscles had become weak and flabby and it seemed that dropping me into a new (new but old

– have I mentioned familiar but surreal?) environment had completely thrown me off my game. This was exhausting. Despairingly, I thought about fleeing back to my couch and under a blanket. I thought about the hundreds of episodes of *RuPaul's Drag Race* that I could revert to, that would spare me this constant internal dialogue.

'I'd like to dive with you.'

Hmm? 'Oh, sorry, can you say that again?' I asked, jolted from wrestling with my thoughts.

'I'd like to dive with you.'

'Me? Oh, right. Great. I'm only getting back in the water, though, and I've no idea how it'll go and … you see, long Covid …'

I hated myself at that moment. I hated the uncertainty, the need to explain, over-explain, justify and vindicate. Why did I feel the need to do that? Couldn't I feel assured and operate from a grounded sense of … I don't know – self?

Get a fucking grip, Claire, I hissed to myself. I looked at Nanna. Her face was warm and open.

Deep breaths, Claire, you're grand.

'Cool, that'd be nice,' I offered tentatively.

'Super, we go tomorrow.'

Tomorrow … super.

chapter 22

UNDER WATER

It turned out, I had no need to worry. My body remembered. All the return-to-Dahab experiences combined to leave me excited, grateful, surprised, softened and in acceptance of what I could do and where I was at that moment. I began to have an inkling that, all these years, I have underestimated myself. Maybe the fights and battles with my body, the harsh words hissed through gritted teeth at my reflection, the punishments of too much or too little food in an attempt to get to grips with something far outside my body's remit, weren't necessary. The struggle of the last year where I, at times, put my fingers in my ears, refusing to hear what my body had to say and instead told it what to do. In retrospect, no wonder there had been no trust between us; communication had broken down completely.

I spent hours and hours playing in the water – diving on the line, floating on the surface, swimming over reefs, twisting and turning underwater in a clumsy but joyful dance – because it felt good, because I was able to. My body remembered. Like my car, which, once I switch off my thoughts, drives itself to Leixlip, home to Ryevale. In the water, I didn't have to think or worry or analyse or plan. Here, my body took over and knew what to do. Underwater I knew how to simply be.

I am so hard on myself – I would do better cutting myself some slack. A sentiment that is often repeated to me by Boudy. But surrounded by the most incredible light of Dahab sunset, the place where Boudy and I had our first date, my body completely supported by warm, salty water, I'll pretend I realised that myself.

On this trip I'd had conversations with divers who'd spoken about time out of the water, either through illness or circumstances or life. These divers, so accomplished, at times had felt pressure, lack of confidence and almost like they had to earn the right to freedive again, to prove that they deserved to dive. Listening to the words spill out in a cascade of honesty and vulnerability, I was shocked. I'd thought it was just me! Plus they were far deeper, far more established divers than I was. I looked up to them. How could they, with all their achievements, still feel like that?

One of these divers was Gary McGrath. I'd met him during my trip in 2020 but it wasn't until I'd got home and followed his progress on social media that his story really piqued my interest.

In 2020, he was training to compete. It was to be his first competition in seven years. Shortly before the competition, I was sitting in Fresh Fish, the afternoon hangout spot, and Gary moseyed up to our table and plonked down on the chair beside me.

'Should you not be at the athletes' meeting?' I said, looking at my watch.

'No, I'm not going to compete.'

'Ah shite, why?' we all exclaimed. Possibly only myself and McGoo using the word 'shite'.

'Something isn't 100 per cent,' he replied, hand pressing the muscles at the top of his chest.

'Wise call. Probably best,' the other, more experienced divers agreed.

I thought it was such a pity. He was all geared up to go; he'd done his training and scheduled it so he'd peak for the competition. It struck me as ego-less, assured and focused on the bigger picture. Fair play.

A few months later, back in the Irish winter, I spotted an Instagram post that he'd reached the BIG milestone for any diver, a depth some of us only dream of. He had dived to 100 metres.

Read that again, 100 metres! In honour of his home place, I'll compare it to a well-known London landmark this time. Big Ben is 96 metres tall. So he dove the height of Big Ben – and a bit!

Incredible! I typed out my congratulations in the comment section and thought back to him a few months previously, holding off. The decision had clearly paid off and I couldn't have been more delighted for him.

That was a time during my experience of long Covid when everything was uncertain. But my head kept on coming back to freediving. Was that it? Was I done? Would I lose the thing I had in common with all my friends dotted around the world? Could I no longer be part of this community?

I was still undergoing tests on my lungs and heart to check for damage from long Covid, but my energy, my small daily allotment of spoons, was the thing prohibiting me from planning my return.

I'd voiced this to Niamh.

'Just pull a Gary.'

'What?' I'd asked. She reminded me of how I'd spoken about the English diver, the admiration I showed for his patience and approach. So, she advised, I should do the same: chip away at the work, put one foot in front of the other and, above all, trust in the timing.

Shortly after I got back to Dahab in March 2022, I met Gary and, over a coffee, told him about pulling a Gary.

Of course, I had to pause for him to make the accompanying jokes and innuendos that the phrase sparked, but I could see it had struck a chord.

This started a series of conversations and, I suppose, a friendship between the two of us. Gary told me his story, about the seven years of not competing and not even freediving. He spoke of similar feelings to ones I had experienced, a sense of loss, not just for the sport but for his identity and for the community that goes with it.

'Did you ever dream that you'd make it to where you are now?' I wanted the formula, to know how he'd maintained his sense of belief, sense of confidence, as all his contemporaries moved past him. If he'd just share his secret ...

'I definitely felt like I'd been left behind but soon it wasn't about that. It was about finding a way back to doing what I love, what we love, because I needed it for me.'

I understood. I didn't bother hiding the tears that trickled down my cheeks. 'Tell me about 100 metres.'

By the time Gary finished describing that epic dive in all its glorious detail – and I wanted to hear every one – we both had tears in our eyes. I won't spoil it in the hope that one day it'll be on paper, in his own book, telling his story. But the presence of mind, the sense of accomplishment and the gratefulness to his partner, Lynne, that had seen him through the whole journey, was the stuff of dreams. More importantly, it was the stuff of hope.

So now, March 2022, he was gearing up to go to Vertical Blue, the most prestigious freediving competition in the world. In a way, he reminded me of me three years previously. Of course, in terms of our abilities it could be likened to comparing a beginner runner at the start of their couch-to-5K journey to an accomplished athlete preparing to run the Boston Marathon. We were leagues apart. But there were the same financial quandaries to figure out, the same waves of doubt and even imposter syndrome. Here was Gary, one of the few elite divers that had dived past 100 metres, and he felt like I had. I had huge admiration for his diving accomplishments, but what struck me was not his abilities in the water, but his humbleness and his humanity on land.

It got me thinking about my own achievements. Just like he'd never *not* be a 100-metre diver, I'd never *not* be the first person to represent Ireland at the World Championships. The achievement isn't necessarily my diving, but that doesn't negate the personal challenge, accomplishment and absolute shove outside my comfort zone. Chatting with Gary, seeing his trajectory and hearing the story of the years that led to his 'overnight success', set off those little 'pings of possibility' in my head, the beginning of dreams before self-doubt comes to rain on your parade. I found my head being turned towards the possibility of what I might achieve one day.

Possibility.

Hope.

Before coming to Dahab in 2022, I had a conversation with someone where they enquired about my health, my long-Covid status. Not waiting to hear my response, they launched into a wine-fuelled speech, pointing out how I was a freediver, even taught breathing classes, and now I was the one having trouble breathing – the sheer irony! Stoney-faced, I listened for a time, barely scraping 'polite' as I excused myself to go to the bathroom and from having to listen further. It got to me. I thought about that evening many times after that, about a carefully worded response that would put an end to having my health used as a punchline, a form of entertainment for the table. I was furious that I had let it get to me so much. I didn't want to admit it, but it had hit home. It had tapped into that underpinning emotion: Fear.

Some time back in the water reminded me, reassured me, that I had long since redefined my relationship with Fear. I now recognised it a little sooner. I was more used to calling it by its name, and though I didn't always welcome the message it came to deliver, I did pay heed to it. After all, some of my best decisions and opportunities had come from a place of fear.

Diving on this trip was different to anything I'd experienced before … or maybe I was different to how I'd been before. The simple pleasure and relief of being back underwater revealed to me that how I felt about freediving had changed. My ambition, my motivation had shifted. Relinquishing the urge to prove myself, to not be left behind, to overcome a perception of weakness had opened up what freediving was to me and more importantly, what it could be. Sunset swims, gliding along the sea floor trying to catch the beams of light that flickered and danced before my eyes, punctuated each day. There was something so simple about the pure enjoyment of kicking down, pulling myself along by rocks below the surface and forgetting about everything else outside that moment. This was time for just me, in my body, below the surface. The line dives and buoys had been a classroom, enabling me to relearn and hone my skills, to test my abilities and discover a strength, resilience and stamina that co-exists beautifully beside a softness, acceptance and an exquisite awareness.

Did I want to compete again? Yes, definitely. I definitely did, but before that I wanted to invest more, explore more. My intentions felt more ... pure? I wanted to find out what I was capable of. I wanted to shine a light into the dark corners and crevices, the things, thoughts and beliefs that held me back. Freediving gave me the space to do that, what is discovered underwater then applied on land. It is my playground for self-exploration and development. I wanted to compete, not to prove things to myself, to others, or to transform my internal struggles and battles into tangible achievements, but to keep challenging and strengthening my relationship with myself and, in turn, how I interacted with the world.

I didn't know how that would look, how it would work out. I suppose, like many before me, I'd have to put one foot in front of the other and trust the timing. But my life had and was working out. I worked and worked as a single woman to create a life of meaning, of that opposite of depression, a life I'd be proud of even if I never found someone to share it with.

But now I had.

In that there's a renegotiation to be made, different elements to consider ... but isn't that the adventure?

EPILOGUE

Now framed, once tucked in the back of the wallet I brought everywhere with me, the poem 'For the Traveler' by John O'Donohue was given to me by my dad. The words of a different John, his message when sending me off on my adventures would become a balm, a beautiful arrangement of sentiments that would describe an experience, my experience, when my own vocabulary failed me.

Soothing as a song, as sacred as a prayer, this poem helped me understand my urge to roam, my pull homewards, and spoke of the part of me that I only seemed to be able to access, to hear when on foreign soil. To this over-explainer who often found herself grappling with reasons and justifications (to herself) why she needed to go, this Irish poet and philosopher shaped verses that told the story I desperately had tried to understand and communicate.

I've spent 36 weeks in Dahab cumulatively over the last five years. I've spent hours on the Turkish Airlines website, looking up flights, daydreaming, playing what-if, comparing prices to the balance in my bank account, wondering if I could swing it.

Dahab has become a refuge. It isn't a magical answer, a place you go to leave all your problems behind, because, ultimately, wherever you go, there you are. But over the years it has become an escape, a chance for the dust to settle and for me to get a better sense of myself.

It's not that it's a desert-style utopia. The facilities and infrastructure are rudimentary, getting sick from the food is par for the course, and there's always a faint musk of camel or goat wee in the air – unless you're near a dive shop, then it's wee-soaked neoprene. One of my favourite games to play when I'm there is 'What would I do if Mum and Dad came to visit? Or Katie or Sarah or Matt?' I plan where they would stay, where I'd bring them to eat and what activities they'd do. But honestly, I think they'd be horrified. It's scruffy. There's no getting away from that. But I know that if I could coax them to put their faces in the water and look at Dahab below the surface, it'd go a long way towards changing their minds.

This trip has been good; it's been different. I'm staying, for the first time, a little bit further out of town. It's quiet, it feels a little bit more authentic, and cycling my bike to and from the centre of town, I can't help but marvel at the changes I already feel being here a few weeks, and more so, the changes in myself since my very first visit five years ago.

In my mind's eye, I catch sight of 34-year-old Claire running across the newly tarmacked street and losing her flip-flop to the tar. Her hair teetering between curly and frizzy in the October heat, she still has a lightness to her. Only weeks in Dahab, she'd settled in, in a manner she never would have anticipated. A bit of colour on your face does wonders for a person, but so does a bit of lightness of the soul.

Thirty-five-year-old Claire walks by, earphones in and talking to herself. Eyebrows furrowed, it's like she's fighting with herself, with the beliefs that have syphoned joy, pride and a sense of accomplishment from her life. That 2018 Claire is feeling every nerve tingling, each pang of the growing pains that comes from knowing what you don't want and enduring the onslaught of pushes back to the small, the comfort zones that go with it. Change is messy and disruptive and will test you as you try to assimilate new ways of doing, thinking and believing. She doesn't realise that it's the beginning. It's the first time she's taking a step forward and thinking, *I deserve more.* Poor 2018 Claire. I wish that the following months were a montage of taking steps in the right direction, shedding remnants of the fear that holds her back. But life seldom works like that ... and progress *definitely* doesn't.

Then 2019 Claire arrives to Dahab on Bambi-like legs. Unsteady but this time something is different: there's a resolve. She's set herself a task that she doesn't know how to get to the end of but she's committed to finding her way through, eating the elephant piece by piece. This Claire knows that whatever unease she feels, the quaking with imposter syndrome, this is her time. She's surrounded herself with structures and tools that set her up for success. She has a fair bit ahead of her, but she's on the right track. The things she learns and the habits she forms this summer will be a comfort, a reminder in years to come that she *can* do it.

And would ya look! She's with a boy – and an Egyptian lad at that! So casual, almost aloof ... I won't tell her and spoil the surprise.

I can *hear* 2020 Claire. No doubt I'll find her in Fresh Fish, squashed in the middle of a large group playing cards. There she is! Oh! She has a good hand ... and a horrible poker face. Watch how she's wiggling in her seat a bit – it gives her away every time. She's so happy to be here. I'm proud of her, her growth, her softness, her stepping into herself. She wants to be the best version of herself and is learning a kinder and more compassionate way to get there. She has let herself be loved by the most unexpected man and his love gives her the security and freedom to roam and enjoy her love for the sport. She misses him, though.

And me. Well, they're all me. But I can see them all so clearly and I want to line all of us up together and pull them in for the tightest bear hug my arms can muster. I want to reassure them, commend their strength and tell them to get out of their own fucking way and just go for it. Sometimes I feel like I need a future version of myself to tell me that.

I've gone out to the desert. We're staying in a campsite on the beach – desert and sea being the most extraordinary combination. Our tents form an L shape that opens out to the water. It's warm during the day and cold at night. Neither matters – our days are spent underwater and the nights we layer ourselves with blankets or warm ourselves by the fire. Boudy would love it. I want to come back here with him some day.

Today we went to some incredible dive sites. Shark Observatory was false advertising, for no sharks did we observe. But we found fish of every colour. One of the divers, Mark, a marine biologist, was able to give us their real names as opposed to my exclamations of 'Oh! A zebra fish. Ha, look at the jazz-hands fish. Look, a ray fish … actually, maybe that's just called a ray.'

It turns out my light sensitivity isn't restricted to land. Looking up to the surface, I get a shot of pain through my eyes and nausea to my stomach. A small part of me is frustrated about not being able to participate fully, the way I want to … but I'm not going to beat myself up about it. I've learned that uttering 'I used to be able to' gets me nowhere other than frustrated. I'm able to do plenty right now. I'm here and nothing will dull the sense of exhilaration at being immersed in this world again.

There's a full moon tonight. They're my favourite. In the cove in Greystones, only a few months ago, in December, Boudy got down on one knee and proposed under a full moon. Waves lapping, stars twinkling, I didn't have to think. I said yes.

Tonight myself and my friends are sitting by the water's edge, under the stars, the light dancing on the surface of the water, sharing a tumbler of whiskey and a joint between us. Just like that night in December, very few things could make this moment more perfect.

It feels like I've brought the Claire's-of-Dahab-past with me, not haunting but providing comparisons, metrics as to how much I've grown. I can feel their presence, their vulnerability, their determination, their fear and their strength. It's all still in me.

I feel older and I'm good with that. This version of me is grounded, softer and certain that there are incredible things waiting for me to step into. In this moment I know how lucky I am. I know how many of my contemporaries at home yearn for this space, this time to themselves. Without feeling the urge to apologise for it or undermine it, I can see why. It is the most magnificent gift. I'm soaking up an experience not quite knowing how it will enhance my thinking, broaden my views and expand my horizons, but I know it will. In this moment, my soul feels at peace.

In a few weeks I will go home to Ireland. The second half of the year is laid out in a series of landmark events. I'll turn 40, we'll get married, *and* I'll even write a book. Maybe next year we'll have a baby – who knows. If there is to be a baby in our lives it'll come to us. *Inshallah*, as my future husband would say.

I'm on the cusp of the next phase, the next set of adventures.

I've grown, I've changed. I've worked so hard to meet my needs and chase my dream, what I thought I wanted. It doesn't go unnoticed that when I let go, when I chased *me* and what ignited the fire in me, that's when things fell into place.

Like most couples, Boudy and I have a song. We laugh every time we hear it. It doesn't connect us to a particular memory, a romantic moment or a point in our relationship. But when I sing along, I often find the words getting caught in my throat, hitting a much deeper part of me, making me smile and tear up at the same time. It sums me up. It sums us up neatly, concisely, perfectly.

Our song is one by the Rolling Stones. Just as the title says – 'You can't always get what you want' – I can't help but close my eyes and smile in recognition, in acceptance that some things may not come as you wish, but they do come exactly as you need.

ACKNOWLEDGEMENTS

Ronan Clinton and Timewise Systems – so many freediving adventures would not have been possible without your support. Thank you for having faith in me … though the earworm war *will* continue!

Niamh 'Queen of Spoons' Reid and Colin 'Believe' McEndoo, thank you for being two bright spots amid the crapness of long Covid.

Aoife McKiernan and Yvonne Leon, for the chats, the vents and for lifting dangerously bottomless champagne glasses with me every step of the way.

Ruth Fitzmaurice, when I asked, 'So how *do you* write a book?', you shrugged your shoulders and said, 'Just write from your soul.' Turns out that was exactly what I needed to hear.

Niall Meehan, always a reliable sounding board, thank you for all the *photo-taking*, the friendship and for being part of this journey from proposal to publication.

To all the cove crew, for sharing sunrises, hugs and away games that have soothed my soul, filled me with joy and made me look around and think, 'This is f***ing deadly!'

Nanna Kreutzman, for literally and figuratively holding my hand as I stepped back into the water. You gave me courage, helped me to believe ... and then captured it all on camera.

Dave McGoo, thank you for answering random freediving questions out of the blue and for the many chats over coffee and all the craic of the past years.

Gary McGrath and Stig Pyrds, thank you for sharing your stories with me. I want to dive like you when I grow up.

To the Dahab folk and freediving friends that I've shared buoys, coffees and card games with. I miss you all.

Mari Rampazzo and Eimear Bradbury, you have been so ridiculously generous with your skills and encouragement. Who would have thought planks and pinches were a form of support?

Lisa Battersby, thank you for listening to every single thought that's passed through my head in the last eight years. Now, put this book down and message me.

Mairin O Shea, it's a particular type of friend that would eat incriminating notes for you. Whatever the forty-year-old equivalent is, I know you'd do it for me. Thank you.

Charlotte and Louise – whether it's puppets, free-diving, travelling or drinking bubbles that are only 11 *fershent*, you don't question but just get on board … and are always ready to cheer the loudest.

Sarah Williams of the Sophie Hicks Agency, thank you for taking a chance on someone who was, essentially, winging it. This book would never have seen the light of day without you.

To the team at Gill, especially Sarah Liddy and Rachael Kilduff, who had the arduous task of following tangents and timelines in earlier manuscripts. Your feedback, patience and approach made rewrites a painless process and, dare I say, enjoyable.

James, Paul and Hannah, thank you for all the videos, quotes and messages sent. They made me laugh, made me think and helped me *keep her lit*.

Robbie, Joy and Ollie, you are too fecking cute for your own good. You crack me up and provide the delightful chaos that brings so much life to our family occasions.

Katie, Sarah and Matt, thank you. Whether it's through slagging, a boot up the arse or raising a glass in Ryevale, you are there for me. I can always rely on honesty and there are few opinions that I value more.

Boudy, thank you for letting me share our story. There's no one I'd rather have done this mad adventure with. *Ana bahebak, Habibi.*

Lastly, to Mum and Dad. You've witnessed every high, every low and everything in between. There are no two people who deserve to share this with me more than you. This is for you.